TRUE
PATRIOT
LOVE

MICHAEL
IGNATIEFF

TRUE
PATRIOT
LOVE

FOUR GENERATIONS IN
SEARCH OF CANADA

VIKING
CANADA

VIKING CANADA

Published by the Penguin Group

Penguin Group (Canada), 90 Eglinton Avenue East, Suite 700,
Toronto, Ontario, Canada M4P 2Y3 (a division of Pearson Canada Inc.)

Penguin Group (USA) Inc., 375 Hudson Street, New York, New York 10014, U.S.A.
Penguin Books Ltd, 80 Strand, London WC2R 0RL, England
Penguin Ireland, 25 St Stephen's Green, Dublin 2, Ireland
(a division of Penguin Books Ltd)
Penguin Group (Australia), 250 Camberwell Road, Camberwell, Victoria 3124,
Australia (a division of Pearson Australia Group Pty Ltd)
Penguin Books India Pvt Ltd, 11 Community Centre, Panchsheel Park,
New Delhi – 110 017, India
Penguin Group (NZ), 67 Apollo Drive, Rosedale, North Shore 0745, Auckland,
New Zealand (a division of Pearson New Zealand Ltd)
Penguin Books (South Africa) (Pty) Ltd, 24 Sturdee Avenue, Rosebank,
Johannesburg 2196, South Africa

Penguin Books Ltd, Registered Offices: 80 Strand, London WC2R 0RL, England

First published 2009

1 2 3 4 5 6 7 8 9 10 (RRD)

Manufactured in the U.S.A.

ISBN: 978-0-670-06972-9

Library and Archives Canada Cataloguing in Publication data available
upon request to the publisher.

Visit the Penguin Group (Canada) website at **www.penguin.ca**

Special and corporate bulk purchase rates available; please see
www.penguin.ca/corporatesales or call 1-800-810-3104, ext. 477 or 474

For my wife, Zsuzsanna, as always

CONTENTS

Author's Note   ix

1   True Patriot Love   1

2   Ocean to Ocean   31

3   After the Somme   71

4   Lament for a Nation   117

5   The Inheritance   155

Notes   179
Primary Sources and Acknowledgments   185
Secondary Sources   189
Index   195

AUTHOR'S NOTE

In 2000, when I began working on this book, I was a private citizen. When I finished it in 2009, I had become a politician. The intentions I had at the beginning—to tell the story of my mother's people and their vision of Canada—were the intentions that carried me through to the end. It is a tribute to my mother, Alison Grant Ignatieff, and is offered to the granddaughter she never got the chance to know, Sophie Turia Ignatieff.

I
TRUE PATRIOT LOVE

True patriot love in all thy sons command.
With glowing hearts we see thee rise,
The True North strong and free!
(FROM "O CANADA!," THE NATIONAL ANTHEM OF CANADA)

I
On the Love of Country

Loving a country is an act of the imagination. We start from what we know—the street where we grew up, the brightly lit skating rinks at night, the tingle of the lake water when we first plunge in, the feeling when we set our feet back on native soil—and we make these parts stand for the whole. What we know is only a fragment of what is there. We have to imagine the expanse we have not seen. We have to imagine the ties that bind us to our fellow citizens, many of whom may not even speak the same language. We reason out from the rituals we share, the rights

3

we enjoy, the traditions we hold in common—and we imagine belonging to a place we can call home. Our political system, the leaders, the laws, the symbols and anthems matter to us because, when they work as they should, they give us the feeling that we share a life in common with the strangers we call fellow citizens.

We engage in this act of imagination because we need to. The lives we live alone do not make sense to us unless we share some public dimension with others. We need a public life in common, some set of reference points and allegiances to give us a way to relate to the strangers among whom we live. Without this feeling of belonging, even if only imagined, we would live in fear and dread of each other. When we can call the strangers citizens, we can feel at home with them and with ourselves. Isaiah Berlin described this sense of belonging well. He said that to feel at home is to feel that people understand not only what you say, but also what you mean. You love the country because it gives you the possibility of feeling at home. You cannot feel this alone. Your emotions must be shared with others in order for them to make any sense at all. A solitary patriot is a contradiction in terms. Love of country is an emotion shared in the imagination across time, shared with the dead, the living and the yet to be born.

Love of country, being imagined, is not a natural feeling like hunger. Human beings invented the complex emotions we feel for nations only in the eighteenth century. What we imagine we can forget. What we dream we can lose. Countries, being human creations, can experience both birth and death.

A country begins to die when people think life is elsewhere and begin to leave. It begins to die when order disintegrates, when people cease to trust their fellow citizens or their government. In a country that is truly alive, the laws hold us in obedience, not just through fear of punishment but also through attachment to the values and traditions the laws protect. If this attachment wanes, if obedience is reduced to fear, either chaos or tyranny beckons.

While love of country has to be shared, the feelings that are shared are not necessarily the same for every citizen. Patriotism is a contested emotion because countries are contested places. Citizens disagree with each other about what the country should stand for, what its traditions mean and what path it should take in the future. These disagreements are intrinsic to the life of any country that calls itself free. If such disagreements weren't a necessary part of public life, we wouldn't need politics. But we do. Politics is how we manage public disagreement without resorting to violence. If our politics is good enough, we can keep our disagreements civil, but that's not to say free of anger. Some of the best patriots I have met have been the angriest. Their love of country expressed itself in fury at some act—a wrongful war, a terrible decision—that they believed betrayed the country's best ideals.

To be a citizen is to belong but also to argue. People will even argue about love of country itself. Some citizens, often the most thoughtful ones, don't love their country and don't believe you should love it either. They don't believe in the emotion itself. They will tell you it is false or made up, even a kind of collective delusion. They will tell you that love of country is old-fashioned and out of style. The world has moved on. Borders are porous. National traditions are no longer self-contained. Cultures are no longer closed to the outside world. Besides, the old national passions brought war and intolerance in their wake. The right emotions to have, they say, are global and cosmopolitan. Why should I feel more for my native land, they say, than I do for Paris, London or New York? These places are the centre of my world. Don't talk to me about your love of country and, whatever you do, don't ram it down my throat.

To be a patriot in the modern age is to be in a perpetual argument with cosmopolitans. The best argument on the cosmopolitan side is that no allegiance—certainly no national identity—ought to claim all of a person. A true patriot should learn from these arguments. The frontiers of a country should never be the frontiers of a person's world. Those unwilling to learn from languages, cultures and traditions beyond the boundaries of their own are in prison, even if they may not notice the bars. From a moral point of view, the strength of the cosmopolitan view is its association with the universal, as opposed to the merely national. The claim of one's country should never be total. A true patriot can always admit the limitations of home. A true patriot can always see the place for what it is.

The best argument on the patriot's side is that cosmopolitan attachments depend on the security countries provide. Cosmopolitanism is the privilege of those with a passport, the luxury enjoyed by those with a country of their own. Those who don't think they need a country, those who believe they are beyond the local attachments of a national state, ought to visit a refugee camp. There they will discover people dying, sometimes literally, to get into a country they can call their own. Statelessness is the very definition of modern hell. Just ask illegal immigrants or people without papers what they want. They want a country.

Countries not only protect us; they provide us with legitimate order. Tyrannies provide the order without the legitimacy. Democracies engender love—and therefore legitimacy—because they ask their citizens to participate in public affairs. The rituals of political participation— voting, campaigning, raising money, standing as a candidate—ought to leave us feeling that we live in a public world that, however imperfectly, reflects the popular sovereignty we exercise with others.

We may not like the decisions that are made in our name, but we know we have a way to change them, and we know who can be held responsible for the mistakes made in our name. The people who make the decisions are no better and no worse than we are. When we feel that the authority exercised in our name is legitimate, we can live with the assurance that the country will cohere and survive into the future. Countries provide us with public meaning, with continuity in time.

To love anyone is to feel responsible for them, to want to watch over and keep them from harm. To love a country is to feel the same, to feel responsible for public affairs, to feel angry when things are going badly, to feel good when things are going well and, above all, to feel that you have some small role in shaping the course of public affairs.

Those who shelter in the protection of their country, those who benefit from legitimate authority, have no obligation to love their country. Attempts have been made to compel people to display their patriotism. The result has been tyranny. Like all forms of love, love of country must be free, or it is nothing but a sham.

All the same, those who freely love their country often feel themselves to be in a retrograde minority. In the face of all the people who believe love of country old-fashioned, or downright dangerous, patriots have to stand up for their convictions. If you are a patriot in the modern world, you have some explaining to do.

You also should be ready to laugh at yourself. There is much, after all, that is ridiculous about patriotism. Parodies of patriotism—Mounties singing "I'm a lumberjack and I'm okay"—sometimes have more life in them than the national anthem. Then there is the embarrassment of standing at attention with fellow citizens you neither like nor trust. You can almost hear them thinking the country would be a better place if it had fewer people like you in it. Yet you stand together, side by side. Solidarity always entails moments like these. Love of country can't endure unless it sees the ironic side of itself.

Yet only so much irony is possible, because love of country is a sentimental and sincere emotion—one that can't afford to be too complicated before it just falls apart. With love of country, you have to keep it simple. You love what you love, and that's good enough for you.

Still, you may also know a lot of things about your country that you have trouble admitting. Patriotism can be expressed in the conditional. If only we had decent leadership. If only we could dig ourselves out of our debts. If only we could extricate ourselves from this war.

People love their country despite a lot of things, despite the president, despite the prime minister, despite some recent scandal, embarrassment, war, famine, conflict, economic disaster. They love it because they haven't given up on it. They love it because of its unrealized possibilities.

We love our country not because we think it is perfect or even satisfactory, but because we think it can change for the better. Love of country requires us to be forgiving of the way things are. Leaders come and go. The people who speak on behalf of the country sometimes let us down. The country itself changes all the time, sometimes for better, sometimes for worse, yet the potential for its redemption endures. This same potential endures in each of us.

A country's past is rarely always glorious, and a true patriot is obliged to be truthful, to acknowledge the dark with the light. The morality of patriotism turns on being both truthful and hopeful at the same time: truthful about the dark passages, hopeful that the light passages promise better days in the future.

We never love a country just for what it is. We love it for what it might yet become. The same is true for the love we bear ourselves. Love is always rooted in hope.

II
Imagining Canada

This is a romantic view of love of country. Sociological accounts of what a country is miss out on the passion that holds countries together and inspires their moments of greatness. This passion is fundamentally a faith in the country's future. In the romantic view, the country that actually exists is a shadow of what it could be. The real country, the object of love and longing, is an imagined place on the horizon that we hope to reach one day, if we can marshal sufficient courage, faith and determination. From this idea of love comes a romantic idea of politics.

According to this idea, the purpose of our political life as a people is to narrow the gap between the land we live in and the land we dream of.

The country in question for me has always been Canada. It is an invented place, created by political leaders one hundred and forty odd years ago, rather than emerging out of the common soil of a shared language and single ethnic origin. Since everything about Canada was invented, everything about it must be reimagined over and over again, lest its founding myths lose their hold on loyalty and faith.

The fundamental challenge of being Canadian is to believe in ourselves. We look in the mirror and see an uncertain and diminished reflection. The story we tell about ourselves is cast in terms of survival and endurance, not triumph. We feel we are lucky to be still here. Given how rich and spacious our land is, given how gently the forces of history have dealt with us, our sense of uncertainty is a puzzle even to ourselves.

We have trouble believing in ourselves because we live next door to a country that has mythic dimensions. It is also an invented country, but its act of self-invention has proven to be the most stupendously successful in history. Canadians can only envy the scriptural sublime of America's Founding Fathers and the self-confidence that the American faith seems to engender in every citizen. In our neighbours' infuriating sense of self-importance, Canadians glimpse how love of country penetrates the souls of its citizens, how profoundly it shapes the character of a people. We wonder why such faith does not inhabit our own souls.

Next to the American experiment, Canada's very identity can appear to be nothing more than what Sigmund Freud once called the narcissism of minor difference. After all, we look like them. We buy the same cars. We dress and talk the same way. We holiday in the same places. We root for the same baseball and football teams. Our differences appear minor and our emphasis upon their importance can seem self-absorbed and trivial. We care more than we should about the distinctive vowel sounds that mark out a Canadian speaking in an American crowd. We care more than we like to admit about beating the Americans at hockey. We know these are small things, but we invest them with defining significance.

We are right to do so. While some of our differences count as minor, others are major indeed. They rebelled against the British. We stayed loyal. They founded a republic. We sought responsible government within the empire. We speak French. They don't.

We owe the Americans much—it's hard to imagine how we could have remained either free or independent had they not too been a free and independent people. But our freedom is different, both in general and in detail: no right to bear arms, north of the 49th, and no capital punishment either. They had the Wild West. We had the Mounties. Rights that are still being fought for south of the border—

public health care, for example—have been ours for a generation. A woman's right to choose is secure here; there it remains contested ground. These differences are major, and the struggle to maintain them, while pursuing ever deeper integration with their richer economy, is the enduring challenge, not just of our identity but of our statecraft.

Establishing a uniting national myth beside a nation as powerful and as supremely gifted at myth making as the United States is never going to be easy. The country that gave us Hollywood and Disneyland casts a glare that makes it hard to see the Canadian shape in the snow.

Besides, we cannot create a single myth, like the United States, because we have three competing ones, English Canadian, French Canadian and Aboriginal. Three peoples share a state without sharing the same sense of the country at all. It is small wonder, then, that we have never been sure we can continue to imagine a common future.

Nearly twenty percent of our citizens are also foreign born, from every country under the sun. Only Australia counts as many foreign-born nationals among her citizens. These Canadians frequently hold passports from other countries and import the attachments, passions and, occasionally, the ethnic and religious rivalries of their nations of birth. The loyalties of new Canadians are complex, transitional, sometimes divided. When granting them citizenship, their new country does not ask them to choose

Canada and renounce all others. Even so, new Canadians have turned out to be among the most devoted citizens in the country. Why? Because we remain a land of hope and opportunity, and new Canadians see in our unfinished destiny an image of their own unfinished destinies.

Despite these challenges, or because of them, most of us are quietly but intensely patriotic. Our nationalism exemplifies the paradox that feeling for a country increases with the difficulty of imagining it as a country at all.

Imagining what we share is not easy. Imagining this land is never just to imagine it as it appears to you alone. It is to imagine it as an Inuit person might see it, a vast white place where the only sign of Canada is the Mountie detachment in the snow-girt command post at the edge of the settlement. To imagine it as a citizen is to imagine it as a resident of Yellow Quill reservation in Saskatchewan would have had to imagine it, this Canada where two half-naked children died in a snow-covered field in the sub-Arctic darkness because their father tried to take the sick little girls to his parents and never made it, and all you can hope is that death was as mercilessly quick as the cold can make it. What does a resident of Yellow Quill imagine, what do we Canadians imagine our country to be, the morning we learn that children have perished in this way? It is surely more than just a tragic story of one family. It is a story about us.

To imagine Canada, you have to walk a mile in the moccasins of others. In other countries, where language, ethnicity and myths of origin are shared, less empathy is required and more simple identification, one citizen to the other, may be possible. Not with us. To imagine Canada as a citizen requires that you enter into the mind of someone who does not believe what you believe or share what matters to you.

You have to imagine the country as a Québécois might see it, a Québécois who never felt attachment to the flag, to Parliament, to the memories of sacrifice that move you, sometimes, to tears. This is a fellow citizen who voted *oui* in referendums in 1980 and 1995 to break up the country, or, as it was presented at the time, to negotiate a new relationship between a sovereign Quebec and the rest of Canada. These referendums were the defining crisis of our recent history. We came within an inch of dissolution. We are still absorbing the lessons of a near-death experience.

One of these lessons is that to survive as a country, we have to imagine what we have trouble understanding. We have no choice. A contract of mutual indifference between French and English will only defer the evil day. We must learn to live together now. The Québécois who lost the two referendums remain fellow citizens of Canada. They may not want to be here at all, and may still dream of independence one day. Yet we must all work together, if only until the next moment of rupture. Those Québécois will have to understand the intensity of an attachment to Canada they do not feel themselves. We all have to understand, if not respect, the dream they live for. To be a citizen of Canada is to imagine the feelings of those who do not believe what we believe. We have to enter into these feelings if we want to keep the country together.

Imagining the feelings of those who disagree with you is one of the duties of citizenship we speak about least. Without the constant effort of imagining the world from the vantage point of races, languages and religions different from our own, we could not identify any common purposes as a country. Political deliberation would become a dialogue of the deaf. It's hard to see how divided societies like ours could have survived without our shared ability to imagine our differences.

In Canada, empathy has to encompass thirty-three million people, with competing and conflicting myths of origin, spread across six time zones, in five distinct economic regions, speaking, at least at home, almost every language spoken in the world and, in public, two official languages. In spite of everything, we have managed to keep this project in being for one hundred and forty years. This is no mean feat and, in a world ravaged by difference, it is our example to the world.

The national anthem we sing together is not the same in each language. In the French we vow that we will "*protégera nos foyers et nos droits,*" while in the English we vow to "stand on guard for thee." We sing the same tune but not the same words, and in this way we acknowledge what divides us, and in acknowledging it, we cross it.

Our treaty relations with Aboriginal peoples also presuppose that we reason together, nation to nation, across the divide of history. The treaty relationship says Aboriginals must be treated as constituent peoples. They cannot be treated just as individual citizens. They were here first. They had their own laws and institutions. The rest of us came as conquerors. Aboriginals accept the new country, but we must deal with them as a people. This is the basic understanding. Of course, this is only the first act of empathy. Others should follow, though they often do not.

If you ask me what I am proud of as a Canadian, it is that we are trying to understand each other across differences that have broken other countries apart. Our enduring exercise of empathy is the example we have to offer. It is the moral meaning of this country.

Countries should have a moral meaning. A country is a common enterprise that calls us out of our solitude. It calls us out of the cocoon of our selves. It appeals to us to be better, to reach out, to trust and to share. The fact that we are only rarely capable of what the country demands of us is not the main point. The main point is that it asks us to try.

Our histories are many, and the histories of French, English and Aboriginal conflict with each other. Our population is spread out across a great lone land. On any rail journey across this country at night in winter, the lights of houses on the snow give way, pretty quickly, to blackness, bleakness and cold. The railway stations are few and far between, frigid lozenges of light cast on snow. We know we have to stick together to make our country work, but there have never been quite enough of us, and we are so different, one from the other, that there is sometimes not enough empathy, not enough imagining together, to hold the common project intact. But the past tells us that we have been here a long time, and that we have prevailed over many difficulties. If that is so, there is still time enough to build the country we imagine. We are still a band of incorrigible romantics. We still believe in that imagined Canada, just beyond the horizon, which one day we could make our own.

III
Four Generations of Canada

Patriotism runs in families. Patriotic sentiment—questioning, declaiming, affirming—runs through my family soundtrack like the refrain of an old song.

My father's people, the Ignatieffs, were Russian political refugees who came to Canada in 1928. As soon as they got off the boat, the five sons fanned out across the country in search of a new start, while their parents settled down in a farmhouse in Quebec, tending a garden and watching their children become trilingual devotees of a new land. For the Ignatieffs, Canada was hope personified, the land of the second chance. The chief ingredient of their love of country was gratitude.

To give the flavour of this, I need only mention my father, who, within six months of his arrival at age seventeen, and against his mother's entreaties, journeyed west, on a CNR rail pass, to lay track in British Columbia. He laid rails in the Kootenay Mountains all summer, jumped into Kootenay Lake to survive a forest fire, threw an axe in a rage at someone who called him a *bohunk,* a term of abuse for Eastern European immigrants, earned a livid red scar above his left knee when the axe was thrown back at him, and returned to his mother that fall, ten pounds lighter and deeply tanned, and a passionate Canadian.

Thirty years later, by then a husband and father of two boys, he took his family across Canada by rail, and one morning, when the train entered the Kootenays, he stood up in the parlour car and commanded silence of us all. "There, do you hear it?" he cried. "What?" his sons asked. "The tracks! The tracks!" The joy on his face as we passed over tracks that he believed, rightly or wrongly, he had laid himself was a lesson in how deeply he associated his own life story with the building of a country.

In *The Russian Album,* a book I published twenty years ago, I told the story of my Russian family. Now it is time to tell a different kind of story about the Grants, the family my father cast his lot with when he married my mother, Alison Grant, in 1945.

This is not the history of her family, but the story of that family's love of their country. Over three generations they conducted a spirited public argument about what Canada was and should be; they argued with each other across time about the country's destiny, and they shaped Canadian public consciousness with their arguments. I belong to the fourth generation, and this book is both a tribute to and a reckoning with that inheritance.

The story begins with George Monro Grant, my great-grandfather. He was principal of Queen's University in Kingston, Ontario, from 1877 until his death in 1902, transforming it from a Presbyterian bible college to a major institution. He was a stupendously energetic Victorian worthy, a Presbyterian clergyman, a devoted husband, a domineering father, an indefatigable public polemicist as well as a friend of two prime ministers, John A. Macdonald and Wilfrid Laurier.

The decisive event of his life occurred in the summer of 1872, when he was thirty-seven years old. With the railway engineer Sandford Fleming, Grant undertook the very first journey ever made by Canadians across Canada from coast to coast, from Halifax to Victoria. The purpose of the journey was to survey the line for the transcontinental railway.

His account of that journey, *Ocean to Ocean,* was the first description Canadians were given of their vast new home, and the book has remained a defining articulation of our national vision. Grant left Halifax in July 1872, unsure if the new Dominion had a future. On his return in late October, he was certain it had a grand destiny.

Its destiny—he thought countries should have destinies—was to serve as a granary, armoury and refuge for the yeomen immigrants, remittance men and working labourers of Britain. When he saw Canada on the map of the world, he saw it as one of the pink dominions stretching around the globe from London to Cape Town, from Vancouver to Sydney.

He was a puzzling paradox: a nationalist imperialist, a passionate Canadian who believed that the country's survival next door to the United States depended on strengthening the British connection. He engaged in rumbustious public controversy with intellectuals who believed that Canada's alternative destiny lay in free trade and eventual assimilation into the United States.

He lived long enough to see this vision enter its defining crisis in the Boer War of 1898, when South Africa dared to revolt against the British Empire and Canada was asked to put down the rebellion. Grant's life ended in 1902, just as his imperial faith was stretched to breaking point.

His son, my grandfather, William Lawson Grant, at first followed in his father's footsteps, lecturing in imperial

British history at Oxford. But with the coming of World War I, his imperial certainties entered their hour of trial. Major Grant fought for the empire at the battle of the Somme, and was wounded and repatriated to Canada, forever changed by his experience. On his return home, he distanced himself from his father's imperial beliefs, becoming a lifelong champion of the first of the post-imperial world institutions, the League of Nations. Principal of Upper Canada College in Toronto, he was the author of the most widely used history textbook in secondary schools in the 1920s. The Canadian destiny for his generation was to make the passage from colony to nation. And so Canada did.

Upon his death, the same skein of reflection was taken up by his only son, George Parkin Grant. As a young Oxford student in Britain during World War II, he had to decide whether to fight for "King and Country" as his father had done. He chose against the weight of family tradition and served instead as an air raid warden in the London docks. There he witnessed the horror of a direct hit on a civilian bomb shelter. In 1942, after suffering a breakdown, he was repatriated to Canada. Out of this crisis, he slowly emerged, a passionately conservative Christian philosopher who, however much he stood against other family allegiances, remained true to the family vocation of public intellectual. In 1965 he published *Lament for a Nation,* a grieving elegy for the Canada his grandfather had dreamed of, as well as a passionate polemic against what the American Empire had done to the Canadian soul.

It is unusual for a single family to sustain, through four generations, one continuous strand of reflection about a single country. What sustained illusion of self-importance propelled us to believe, generation after generation, that Canadians would care what we thought, would listen to what we had to say? Our Canada, after all, was not the Canada of the French, the Aboriginals or the new immigrants. It was white Anglo-Saxon Canada, and we made a myth of it and passed it off as if we had the right to speak for the whole country.

I can see how vain and distorted our family myth making could be, but for all that, I cannot disavow it. It is part of me.

It is impossible to overstate how present, how alive these three generations were in my childhood. George Monro Grant was the most remote, being farthest away in time. But there was Grant Hall at Queen's, and in the Queen's Archives, one day, while I was looking for something else, I came upon a box that, when its contents tumbled onto the desk, turned out to be three perfectly preserved rolls of birchbark, the size of foolscap. On them I could make out line after meticulous line of a sermon in my great-grandfather's hand. As for my grandfather, there was Grant House at Upper Canada College, where he lived and where my mother grew up in the 1930s, and where I was a boarder in the early 1960s. Even thirty years later, there were old masters who still remembered "Choppy" Grant. There was my grandmother's house at 7 Prince Arthur Avenue in Toronto. That house—long since flattened to make way for the Park Hyatt Hotel—was a carpeted treasure trove of mysterious links to the past. Dresser drawers revealed shell fragments from bombs that fell on London in 1917 and even a fragment of aluminum fuselage from a Zeppelin downed in an early air raid. There were wooden animals from Africa—zebras, lions and wildebeests—brought back from my great-grandfather Sir George Parkin's visit to South Africa in 1903.

Choppy Grant died twelve years before I was born, yet he made occasional appearances, like a departed shade, in the memories of his daughters. My mother remembered him wrapping her up in a blanket at the cottage at Otter Lake and taking her out on an August night, sitting on his shoulders, to see the stars. The names she taught me as a child—Cassiopeia, the Polar Star—were the ones he taught her.

I recall one afternoon in Vancouver thirty years ago when my aunt Margaret, my mother's older sister, drove me to the airport and I began asking her what Choppy had been like. She said that what she valued most about him actually was how ordinary he had been. I looked over and there she was, gripping the wheel, staring straight ahead, tears flowing down beneath her glasses onto her cheeks.

As for my uncle George, my mother's brother, he was a huge presence in my childhood: gigantic, shambling, dishevelled, smoking cigarette after cigarette, but so engrossed in his talk that he would not notice as the ash fell upon the lapels of his jacket. He was by then a famous man, known for his programs on CBC radio and television, and for the infamous *Lament*.

He was a notorious public scourge of liberals, whether big L or small L, and he knew me to be both, so his gentleness with me required rare forbearance. We disagreed about everything, but I found him irresistible and magnetic. It was hard not to be entranced by someone who sang out loud to operas on the stereo and, after motioning for reverent silence whenever the quintet in Mozart's *Cosi fan tutti* was sung, bent his head and listened in tears.

Given this family, given its presence in my early life, the question for me was always: What can I add? Is there anything of my own to say? It has taken me a long time to figure out what that might be.

Nine years ago, long before I went into politics, I began to reassemble the skein that linked the three generations of Grants together. I reread their works, tracked down the voluminous Grant-Parkin correspondence in Canada's national archives and travelled the country with my wife, following my great-grandfather's journey in *Ocean to Ocean*. One continuing theme emerged from my search for their traces. The crux of the family obsession was always, Is there enough here? Is there enough to make a great country?

The Canada the Grants conjured up was never the one that was before their eyes. It was always a Canada they imagined in the future, a Canada yoked to some greater destiny or a Canada, in the case of Uncle George, irreparably lost in the past. If they pushed themselves forward as commentators and public intellectuals, it was because they believed the country needed them, needed the shaping act of the imagination that only they could provide. Yes, such self-importance was ridiculous, but it is what they believed and it is what I inherited.

The starting point they all shared was that Canada alone—the stump-filled fields, the small brick-built towns, the lonely expanses of prairie between the station stops— was not enough. These places became grand, became worth caring about, because their stars were hitched to something greater: the emerging global civilization of an empire on which the sun, as the saying went, never set.

The empire was much more than power, dominion and technology. It was also an ideal of progress, Christianity and the slow and steady spread of the good. George Monro Grant could be as scathing as his grandson about the rapacity and violence of empire—but its failings were, in his eyes at least, incidental. The ways of empire were the ways of God.

The deeper ambiguity in this nationalism—and it was a passionate and proud Canadian nationalism—lay in the proposition that Canada would be forever a provincial and insignificant sketch unless set within the magnificent gilt frame of empire. When the empire foundered in the First World War, the limitations of the imperial vision became all too apparent. The dominions bled on the fields of France, and the bright narrative of Canada marching hand in hand with Britain to global dominion now seemed like a poor delusion. When Major William Lawson Grant returned to Canada, the narrative he created for the country was its organic emancipation from empire, its passage from colony to nation.

Even here, the history was shadowed by the same doubt that had haunted his father's vision: Is there enough here? If the story is the passage from colony to nation, what will our independence be worth when we get it? Once the frame of empire is removed from the picture, what significance will still attach to the sketch of a country that remains?

My grandfather left this question for his son to answer, and the despairing answer came thirty years later in *Lament for a Nation*. Canada had gone from colony to nation to colony, without any autonomous period of true freedom in between. But this was not all. In the era of technological modernity, love of country was a sentimental and retrograde illusion. A place like Canada, George Grant argued, could no longer serve as an object of love and longing.

I rebelled against this pessimism then, as I still do today. But his pessimism lays down the gauntlet. There is no easy answer to the challenge posed by George Grant, for he asked, as no one had ever done before, Is Canada possible? These are all serious questions, and the way to take them seriously is not to give them easy answers.

My own life exemplifies these questions. I grew up in a Canadian household where my parents did think that life was elsewhere. This is how it is in small countries and provincial societies everywhere in the world. My mother used to go about the house humming a Judy Garland song with a line about how, if you haven't played the Palace, you might as well be dead. The Palace Theatre was elsewhere— not in Ottawa, where I grew up, but in the big bright world beyond. So the family question wormed its way into how I thought of my life, and the answer I gave myself was to get out of here, to go out into the bright world beyond and play the palace.

I played the palace in London for twenty years, as a journalist and writer, and for five years at Harvard as a professor. And then I did what they all did—my great-grandfather, my grandfather, my uncle: I came home. Life was elsewhere all right, but this place was my place, my problem, my obsession, my home. The questions my family had always asked—Is there enough here? How do we make this place worthy of our dreams? How do we fix what is so obviously wrong?—those questions became my own. It's why I came back. It's why I entered politics. It's why I'm here.

The spiritual task is to deepen love for a country that remains incomplete. The political task is to narrow the gap between the country we actually live in and the country we imagine. This is the task three generations of my family set itself, and now it is my turn to try.

The best way to begin is to get our bearings, to return to the past and to explore again what these Canadians once believed their country's destiny to be. For what is inspiring about this—and so necessary for us now in our more skeptical half-light—is that our ancestors thought our destiny could be glorious indeed. The best reason to return to the past is that we often discover our ancestors believed in us and our future more than we do ourselves.

One morning in mid-August 1872, when my great-grandfather stood waist high in the grass and looked out at the prairie, somewhere in what is now southeastern Manitoba, alive with songbirds and open to the wide horizon, empty of every human soul, he thought he could see a mighty nation arising here—farmers and labourers, populating these gigantic plains, feeding the world and powering a country to a great place in the world of nations. The mere sight of that empty plain convinced him, he later said, that he had been wrong to doubt the future of Canada. Now he could see the bright horizon. It is good to see that horizon through his eyes, even if the future has come to pass, and is not as bright as he thought. For without this faith, this ancestral belief that we are capable of great things, love of country will die.

2
OCEAN TO OCEAN

I

The Grants emigrated from lowland Scotland to Pictou County in Nova Scotia in 1826. Of the founding father, James Grant, we know only that he was an unsuccessful farmer who married the more considerable figure, Mary Monro, in 1831 and had three children. My great-grandfather, George Monro Grant, was born in 1835. At the age of nine, while playing with other boys in front of an open-cast coal mine near Stellarton, he thrust his hand into the maw of a threshing machine and lost all the fingers of his right hand. Coal miners carried him home, one of them calling out "I have the fingers, Geordie, I have the fingers!" In 1844 in colonial Nova Scotia, the fingers were never going to be sewn back, and George was lucky to escape with his life. His mother slowly nursed him back to health and he became, as might be expected, her special treasure. Perhaps because of this, he came to think of his injury as a blessing in disguise.

The loss of full use of his hand also made him unfit for farming, so after a time at Pictou Academy, where he did well, the Presbyterian church offered him a scholarship to study in Scotland if he would come back to serve the kirk afterward. This he did, returning in the early 1860s, and he soon received a call from the congregation of the St. Matthew's Church in Halifax, where he became the minister.

His faith was optimistic, earnestly practical and, within the limits of the day, enlightened. He hated anti-Catholic sectarianism and stood against the dourest elements of Presbyterianism. He always remembered, with a shudder, the kirks of his childhood, where the men and women sat apart with bowed heads and hell and damnation poured forth from the pulpit in thick Gaelic. His favourite biblical text was St. Paul's Epistle to the Galatians Chapter Five, which begins with the ringing exhortation "Stand fast, therefore, in the liberty wherewith Christ hath made us free." Faith was freedom, the freedom to choose the path to salvation. Perhaps it was not a coincidence either that there was an echo of Galatians in the Grant family battle cry, descended from the Scottish clans of old, "Stand fast, Craigellachie!"

He was a riveting preacher, clear, direct, hopeful and gentle with sinners. The walls of St. Matthew's, the gloomy establishment on Barrington Street where he was minister between 1863 and 1877, still display a plaque put up by grateful parishioners. He was a sought-after dinner guest, and at one such a dinner he met Jessie Lawson, daughter of one of the founders of the Bank of Nova Scotia. He married Jessie, a quiet, frequently bedridden woman of deep intelligence, whom he consulted about everything. They had two sons together, and the tragedy of their lives was the death of Geordie, their youngest, a handicapped child who perished of typhoid at the age of twelve.

Grant proved to be an often absent but unquestionably affectionate husband, writing his wife daily and calling her in his letters "Dear Mother," "My Darling Wife," and signing himself "Your Always Devoted Husband." When he was on the road, his remaining son, my grandfather, always received a special letter, written in large letters so the child could comprehend.

Grant was soon a coming man, a frequent contributor to the newspapers of the day, where in 1866 he argued that the colony should confederate with the rest of Canada. He took on his idol, Joseph Howe, the colonial orator who in 1848 had secured responsible government—quasi-independent status—for Nova Scotia, the first British colonial territory to do so. Howe saw nothing to be gained from confederating with the rest of Canada, and much to lose.

My great-grandfather won this argument for Canada, and he was to win many others. In photographs, he cuts a striking figure: five foot nine in height, slim and wiry, with thinning hair, dressed in a clergyman's black suit and white collar, the stump of his right hand hidden inside a black glove. His eyes radiate vitality, self-confidence and humour. His failings, by his own account, included shortness of temper, irritability and a tendency to drive himself to exhaustion.

In his congregation at St. Matthew's, Halifax, was an equally passionate proponent of Confederation, Sandford Fleming, the prosperous railway engineer who was overseeing work on the building of the Intercolonial Railway that was to link the colonies of the Atlantic with the colonies on the St. Lawrence. Grant and Fleming formed a lifelong partnership, at once political and personal. Both were canny Scots, indefatigable, self-possessed, big men in small ponds, determined to make their marks, devout Christians and, most importantly, romantic adventurers with a touch of the permanent adolescent.

It was Fleming who had the crazy idea of being the first Canadians to journey ocean to ocean. Prime Minister John A. Macdonald had secured British Columbia's entry into Confederation with the promise of a railway, and Fleming was determined to be the man to build it. He had got himself appointed as engineer in chief and wanted to survey the line himself. But he knew that railways meant politics and politics required propaganda. When he listened to Grant's sermons, Fleming knew he had found the propagandist he needed. Before they set out, Grant and Fleming agreed that Grant should write a book. They even agreed on the title and Fleming promised Grant $400 for a completed manuscript. Fleming would demonstrate that the railroad was practicable. Grant would demonstrate that it was irresistible.

Still, they were rank amateurs, and crossing Canada was a risky scheme. Just consider what such a journey involved in the summer of 1872. You'd begin with a train from Halifax to Pictou on the Northumberland Strait. From there, a steamer would take you up the St. Lawrence to Trois Rivières. From there you transferred to the Grand Trunk, which took you to Montreal, then to Toronto and finally to Collingwood on the southern shore of Lake Huron. That was where Canada ended, at least as far as the railway was concerned.

From Collingwood, a steamer would take you through the Great Lakes to Port Arthur at the western tip of Lake Superior. At this point, just halfway across the continent, modern forms of transportation gave way to the horse, cart or canoe. Ahead of you stretched a thousand miles of the Canadian Shield's best swamp, forest and rapids. After that, a further thousand miles of winding tracks through the prairies. After that, the cliff faces of the Rockies barred your way to the ocean. If you wanted to create a country, this was what you had to conquer. The Americans had done it, driving in the last spike of their railway in 1869. If they could do it, Fleming and Grant believed, so could Canadians.

So let us begin that journey where the steamer left them, on the rickety wooden dock at Port Arthur, now Thunder Bay, at first light on July 22, 1872. Besides Grant, the expedition consisted of the rotund figure of Sandford Fleming, his teenage son Frank, a botanist named Macoun, whom they had picked up on the steamer, and Dr. Moren, a mild Halifax physician who was there to keep them healthy. Luggage and provisions were loaded onto carts and the party set off on the Dawson Road, a narrow single track of logs laid across muskeg through dense, wet woods. At Shebandowan Lake, the next morning, everything was loaded into three freight canoes, their birchbark seams caulked with black pitch. Each canoe had a name, *Beaver, Sun* and *Buffalo,* and each came with a steersman fore and aft.

Fleming had engaged two Metis and two Iroquois traders to guide them to Lake of the Woods. They showed up for work in British regimental jackets, grey tunics with brass buttons, white cotton shirts and woollen trousers held up with a coloured Metis sash. They had all been in the service of Sir George Simpson, the legendary governor of the Hudson's Bay Company, in the days when the Bay owned the entire Canadian North West. The staple of the trade, the beaver, was vanishing—and these men, now in late middle age and making their living by paddling settlers west to the plains, were the aristocrats of a trade in its final hours.

Grant settled into the middle of a canoe with Ignace behind and Louis in front, and they set off at a brisk pace through the complex system of portages, rapids, lakes and rivers that led from the western end of the Great Lakes to the Lake of the Woods and the western plains beyond.

For the next eight days, they shot rapids, toted the canoes through long portages or surged through the rivers at dusk, the paddles keeping up a steady stroke. When the rivers broadened out into a lake, the guides would shout "hi hi" and race each other to the night's landing place, where the canoes would be pulled out, turned over and repaired. They were noble company, these Metis and Iroquois steersmen. When they came out of their tents in the morning, Grant noticed, they washed themselves meticulously and re-braided their pigtails. When he held his first Sunday service on a large rock in the middle of one of the rivers, they sang the hymn "Veni Creator Spiritus" in the Iroquois language.

As they journeyed toward the Lake of the Woods, Grant and Fleming met Ojibwa people, fur traders on their last legs, miserably poor, dressed in ragged European jackets embroidered with beads, holed coins and bear claws, sometimes wearing French kepis of buffalo skin decorated with feathers. The women in their camps, Grant noticed, were "dirty, joyless-looking and prematurely old," while the men hunted, fished and did any work "that a gentleman feels he can do without degradation." When the party of white men showed up at these encampments, the language of greeting—as the language of the fur trade had been—was French: "B'jou, B'jou!" (*Bonjour! Bonjour!*). At one encampment, the chief treated them to a magnificent speech in Ojibwa in which, while he welcomed them to his land, he wanted something in return for their passage through it. Grant and Fleming's Iroquois cook prepared the chief a breakfast of fried pork and pancakes and served it on a newspaper spread over a rock.

At night, by the campfire, Grant filled his diary with long reflections in pencil. When the Americans were building the railway, attacks by the Sioux and the Cheyenne on survey parties like theirs had been constant. Grant was relieved that the chief had allowed them passage through his land, but he was aware that he was in the middle of nowhere, utterly dependent on Aboriginal companions whose way of life the railway would eventually destroy. Already, the Ojibwa, having lost the fur trade, were watching from their encampments as white settlers in canoes and barges moved past them, almost every day, on their way to the plains. In his diary, Grant struggled with the realization that his nation would be built on the ruins of others:

And now a foreign race is swarming over the country, to mark out lines, to erect fences, and to say "this is mine and not yours," till not an inch shall be left the original owner. All this may be inevitable. But in the name of justice, of doing as we would be done by, of the "sacred rights" of property, is not the Indian entitled to liberal, and if possible, permanent compensation?

At the Northwest Angle, a landing stage on the western shore of the Lake of the Woods, the Metis and Iroquois guides deposited the party and with a wave of farewell set off back to Shebandowan.

The baggage was loaded onto Red River carts and the party set off, once again, on the Dawson Road, in the driving rain, through thick forest. At two in the morning, soaked and exhausted, unable to see where they were going, they blundered toward a half-finished Hudson's Bay store, left open, and, fumbling past stacks of tools and piles of lumber, threw themselves down and fell fast asleep.

The next morning—July 31st—Grant awoke, rubbed his eyes and stepped out into bright sunshine. They had broken through the forest cover and he was standing on the edge of the Prairies.

"I found myself in Paradise," Grant scribbled excitedly into his diary.

A vast whispering ocean of green grass, waist high, sprinkled with wildflowers, yellow, lilac and white, stretched to the horizon, perfectly flat, under a vast blue sky. The elemental stillness was broken only by the whispering grass and snatches of birdsong. There was not a building, not a fence, not a column of smoke in sight.

That July morning in 1872, he later recalled, was a moment of ecstatic confirmation, one of the happiest of his life. He and Fleming had come west, he later said, "simply to find out whether Canada was doomed to end in Lake Huron, or whether there was a country for our children here and all the way to the Pacific." That day, in July, he said, "the question I had been asking myself was settled."

Fleming, the botanist Macoun and Grant dug around in the soil under their feet and happily, if rashly, concluded that you could stick a plough in here and run a straight furrow all the way to the Rockies. Already, in his mind's eye, Grant began to people the plain with the citizens of a great nation.

The point where they broke the forest cover and encountered the Prairies for the first time is about thirty miles from Fort Garry, what today we call Winnipeg. The waist-high grass is long gone, replaced by close-cropped grazing land, and the silence is gone too, replaced by the flat whine of the big rigs rolling along the four lanes of the Trans-Canada Highway. But you can still feel the wonder my great-grandfather felt when you break through the forest cover of the Canadian Shield and the big sky suddenly opens up and the plains appear, stretching away as far as the eye can see. It is one of the places where Canada awakens awe.

They put the horses back in the shafts and made haste to Fort Garry, arriving in the late afternoon, filthy, fly-bitten and exultant. At the mansion of Governor Archibald, the staff drew them hot baths and gave them their first mail from Halifax. Grant wrote back to his wife, "This is going to be a great country and I am glad that I will hereafter be in a position to know and understand it."

Fort Garry was the bustling administrative centre of Manitoba province, with a straggling village called Winnipeg growing up around it. On the muddy streets, Grant reported, saloons were more numerous than churches. The saloons were full of land speculators, government surveyors divvying up the land into sections and plots, Metis guides and drovers, American railway prospectors, new immigrant farmers and the occasional Cree or Ojibwa.

The new province of Manitoba, brought into the Dominion two years earlier, in 1870, was a tinderbox of resentments. In 1869, Louis Riel, a twenty-eight-year-old former seminarian, had assembled a crowd at St. Boniface Cathedral to protest the presence of federal land surveyors who were, he cried, stealing land from underneath the feet of the Metis. Riel's first rebellion soon took fire, drawing support from English and French settlers alike, and he formed a provisional government and issued a list of demands addressed to the federal government in Ottawa. These included provincial status for the territory, French as an official language of the province, land grants to be controlled by the province, treaties to be concluded with the Indians and education to be controlled by Catholic and Protestant churches. For a time, Riel carried all before him, but when the provisional government hanged Thomas Scott, an English farmer, for resisting, Orange Protestants in Ontario were so outraged that the federal government dispatched a military expedition to put down the insurrection. Riel fled into the Dakota territory.

Grant never met Riel, and for obvious reasons *Ocean to Ocean* avoids any mention of the rebellion. It was essentially a railway promotion brochure, after all, and the less said about rebellions the better. Grant wanted the West to be peopled by white, English-speaking farmers. Riel wanted the West to be French and Metis and Aboriginal. *Ocean to Ocean*'s national dream prevailed. To this day, Riel awaits acknowledgment as the true founder of the province of Manitoba. He remains the apostate visionary of a Canada that never stood a chance.

In Fort Garry, while they were purchasing what they needed for their westward journey, Grant met the leader of the francophone community in Manitoba, the Archbishop of St. Boniface, Alexandre-Antonin Taché, and he sounded out the veteran missionary, probably in French, about whether the land to the west was suitable for agricultural settlement. Taché, sensing that Grant was there to attract droves of English-speaking settlers, avoided giving a clear answer, though the old fox knew the West like the back of his hand.

Grant also met Donald Alexander Smith, Chief Commissioner of the Hudson's Bay Company in the North West, a fellow Scot and Presbyterian, former fur-trade dealer turned railway speculator. Smith, better known later on as Lord Strathcona, became the driving financial force behind the completion of the CPR.

Around midday on August 2, the expedition set off again, a line of Red River carts and buckboards, loaded high with tents, baggage, pemmican, salt pork, pots and pans, guns and ammunition. Occasionally, as they wended their way through the single-track trails of the grasslands, they would pass a new homestead. The last one, some-where near Portage la Prairie, was inhabited, it so happened, by a family called Grant. They had supper with the family in their rough log cabin, one wall decorated with a cheap poster of the Liberal leader of the day, Alexander Mackenzie. Needless to say, these Scottish pioneers, patriotic, Liberal in politics and undaunted by life on the edge of nowhere, enchanted Grant.

George Monro Grant left them thinking noble thoughts, but there was no disguising the fact that beyond that homestead at Portage, there was nothing: not a house or settlement, not a beckoning plume of smoke from a chimney. For the next three weeks, the Prairie sky swallowed them up.

Their imaginations had been prepared by the popular watercolours of Paul Kane depicting romantic Indian warriors spearing buffalo, but there were no warriors and no buffalo to be seen anywhere. The animals had been pushed to the brink of extinction, and the Plains Cree, through contact with settlers and whiskey traders, were being devastated by smallpox and alcohol. Now the railway was coming. Without realizing what they were doing, the Fleming-Grant survey party was sounding the death knell of a Plains civilization that had endured for millennia.

The survey party was in the hands of a Metis guide and a group of Metis horsemen, wranglers and carters, some French, some English, all given to swearing like troopers but all skilled in the ways of the trails that wended their way through the grass, the clumps of alders and the salt ponds day after day for three weeks. The expedition lived on pemmican—dried meat mixed with tallow—and on the fowl that Fleming's son brought down with a shot gun. They made thirty to forty miles a day on the Yellowhead trail, a meandering cart track that connected Hudson's Bay fort to Hudson's Bay fort and led eventually to the Yellowhead Pass in the Rockies.

Apart from summer storms that came upon them in tempests of wind and hail, nothing broke the silence of their days, Grant sometimes lying in the bottom of a wagon gazing skyward, sometimes riding a horse, gripping the pommel of his saddle with the stump of his right hand. In Fort Garry, they had jettisoned their eastern woollens and flannels and now wore riding chaps, boots and buckskin jackets. It's fair to say that those long days on the trail, sometimes breaking into a gallop to run after birds, sometimes chasing each other, other times letting the reins free so that they could daydream, were the happiest moments of my great-grandfather's life.

Once, they stopped in fear as a party of horsemen suddenly appeared on the horizon and rode fast toward them, drawing up in a huge plume of dust. They were Sioux warriors, about eighty of them, chased north into Canadian territory by the railway men, ranchers, settlers and cavalry of the United States. The warriors sidled up beside Grant and Fleming's wagons and, through the Metis guides, told them that they were from the Missouri territory, heading to Fort Garry to swear allegiance to the Great White Mother. Their fear, they told Grant, was that the local Cree and Ojibwa might drive them back into the United States. They were magnificent men, Grant wrote, dressed in blankets and leggings and wearing their eagle headdresses. One of them had a painted tin horse a foot long hanging on his naked chest, skunk fur on his ankles, hawk feathers in his hair and a great bunch of sweet-smelling lilac bergamot flowers under one arm. The chief wore a necklace of bear claws, and moccasins belted with broad stripes of porcupine quills dyed bright gold. They parlayed with Grant and Fleming's party, Grant recorded, "with a dignity of manner that whites in the new world must ever despair of attaining," and then took their leave.

Somewhere in the Saskatchewan territory, they overtook a missionary, George McDougal, and Souzie, his Cree guide, and for a number of days, McDougal and Souzie travelled with them. McDougal was returning to his mission at Victoria Settlement. He had ministered to the Crees there, in a rough-hewn church, dispensary and school, and two years before had lost his wife and his daughters to a smallpox epidemic that had cut down the settlement. To this day, you can see the pitiable marble headstones of the McDougal family, including their adopted Cree daughter, all swept away in what to devout believers must have been the most unfathomable of God's mysteries. Only now was the widower missionary returning to his post. By the campfire at night, the Presbyterian and the Methodist had time to ponder the ways of God.

When Grant asked McDougal to name "any positive improvement in morality that had resulted from the Missionaries' labours," McDougal tersely replied—one can imagine him staring darkly into the campfire—"Yes, Christianized Crees would not steal your horses ... when you were passing through their country."

Come now, Grant insisted, there must be some more positive impact to the Christian message. McDougal would concede only that they "did keep the Lord's Day after a fashion, treated their women rather better, were more comfortable, a little cleaner, sent their children to school for a while." Then he added, bitterly, that they still remained "dirty, vicious, miserable" and not much better than the Indians who stayed pagan. McDougal's despair did not manage to unsettle Grant's optimism. When they did reach Victoria Settlement, Grant was moved to tears by the sight of Cree children singing Christian hymns in their own language.

Grant concluded there were only three alternatives for dealing with the Indians. The Americans had tried the first alternative—extermination—and it had only provoked bloody wars. The second alternative was pauperization, forcing Indians onto reservations as permanent wards of the federal government. This would have the same effect, he thought, as welfare dependency among the white working poor. He remained opposed, throughout his life, to the reserve system. His preferred third way, very vague and high-minded though it was, was to treat the Indian "as if he had in him the makings of a man." When civilized, he added, he will not be like the average Ontarian. "Neither is the French habitant nor the Hindo ... yet both are very good people in their way. But he will be a man." Civilization meant allowing Indians to own property, to become industrious farmers and mechanics like white people did. They could keep treaty lands as communal property, but they should be afforded the incentives of private ownership and hold title to their individual farms and homesteads.

Civilization in his view also meant industrial schools of the type used to educate the working class. The first residential schools for Aboriginal children were established in the 1870s. Canada has lived with the consequences—the legacy of physical brutality, sexual abuse and forced acculturation—ever since.

From Fort Ellice to Fort Carlton, from Fort Carlton to Fort Pitt, the convoy travelled northwest across the plains through the hot days of August 1872. Fleming took careful note of every topographical feature that would have to be overcome when the railway came through. Every Sunday, they rested, repaired the wagons, turned the horses loose, lay in the grass and slept, served themselves extra rations and concluded the day with prayer service. The day of rest, Grant thought, brought the men together, eased the quarrels and ill feeling that grew up during the week, and raised the moral tone, though he confessed he still couldn't get the Metis horsemen to stop swearing.

At Fort Edmonton, a rough plank square that they reached in late August, they all had their photographs taken in their Plains gear, young Frank with a porkpie hat on his head and a carbine under his arm, Fleming with grey beard billowing out from his cheeks and a French kepi on his head, a bearded Grant, in wide riding chaps and a buckskin coat, covering the stump of his right hand with a broad-brimmed leather cowboy hat, and Moren, the doctor, dressed Metis style with a broad, coloured sash holding up his riding breeches. They look about as happy as men can be.

At Fort Edmonton, they switched the gear from Red River carts to pack horses for the mountains ahead. Forty miles out of Edmonton, on the trail to Jasper, they took on new Metis guides and packers. Their destination, the Yellowhead Pass, was named after a legendary French fur trader whom the Indians called Tête Jaune, the blond one. Fleming's plan was to meet up with a survey party led by Walter Moberly, who had started out from the Pacific in June and was surveying the approaches from the other side of the Rockies.

The next month, two weeks up to Jasper and two weeks from Jasper down to the Fraser, was the toughest of the trip. The trails zigzagged upward through miles of bog and tightly packed pine forest. The way was blocked by deadfall or rushing water. The footing was poor; horses went lame, kicked over the traces and dumped their packs. The inclines grew steeper every hour. It rained, and the nights grew colder. Ice formed on their water buckets. On the Prairies, Fleming reckoned, they had made forty miles a day. Now they were down to ten if they were lucky, sometimes fewer than that, and if they didn't keep up speed, they might be caught in the mountains by the winter snow. At Jasper, they failed to rendezvous with Moberly, which put Fleming in a foul mood. Still, they stripped a spruce overhanging the river and drove a railway spike into the base. It is still there.

Finally, they made it to the Yellowhead Pass, a meadow at thirty-seven hundred feet of elevation, framed by peaks on all sides. As soon as they saw it, Fleming knew the railway should go through this pass and no other. The elevation was low and the valley was wide enough that no blasting would be necessary. In celebration they rested and Grant preached a sermon of thanksgiving.

Next day, they reached the Continental Divide, the rivers behind them flowing north to the Arctic, the rivers ahead of them flowing toward the Pacific. More days of miserable slogging ensued, as they struggled down the slopes of the Rockies, along treacherous, slippery trails that had a way of disappearing or running them in circles, all in increasing cold and teeming rain. By this time, they were battling exhaustion and some measure of homesickness. But their spirits lifted when they finally reached the Fraser. At the junction where the Clearwater River meets the Thompson, they bade farewell to their guides and packers and boarded scows and set off down the Thompson toward Kamloops. They camped that night short of the settlement in one of the meadows in a bend of the river, their sixtieth encampment since Lake Superior, and their last.

As the scows were rowed down the river, Grant observed the Indian camps on the shores. Smallpox had swept through the valleys, decimating the people who made their life along the river. The survivors Grant observed in sweat lodges—steam rising from tents where, around a circle of heated stones, the people would sit breathing in the steam, purifying their bodies and their souls. He also noticed how elaborate the Indian graves were: structures made of poles containing the valuables of the deceased, guns, blankets, food, shawls and flags, canoes and painted images of the dead.

Arriving at the Hudson's Bay post in Kamloops, the travellers were treated to their first feather bed in a month. At the Sunday service, where Grant gave a sermon, he had a glimpse of the complex racial and ethnic hierarchy of British Columbia. The British colonial elite were a decided minority. The congregation consisted of American prospectors, farmers (who left their Indian wives outside) and the Chinese. The Chinese had come north after the end of construction of the Union Pacific. Already there was strong prejudice against the Asians in Kamloops, a prejudice, Grant tartly observed, that seemed to ignore that they were "cleanly, orderly, patient, industrious and above all cheap." All his life he was to be a vigorous opponent of anti-Chinese legislation, especially the anti-Chinese immigration quotas. While any state had the right to "keep out bad people," he wrote, "no nation has the right to keep out the good of one nation while admitting both the bad and good from other lands."

They journeyed onward to the sea, taking a steamer from Yale to New Westminster, sharing the trip with the legendary chief justice of British Columbia, Matthew Begbie, who had imposed rough justice on the gold fields, Indian settlements and backwood camps, armed only with a couple of constables and the criminal law of England.

Arriving in New Westminster, Grant and Fleming were greeted as celebrities by the governor, who put at their disposal a steam vessel that they used to explore the coast for the next two weeks. The key question was what place to choose as the eventual terminus of the railway. Was it to be Bute or Burrard Inlet? The local politicians, the governor and the assemblymen all wanted to know—but Fleming kept his counsel as the little steamer methodically plied its way through Howe Sound, down into English Bay and along the Spanish Banks. Apart from a sawmill here and there, there was nothing but primeval forest and silence in the vast inlet surrounded by mountains. The silent, green-flanked harbour Grant sailed through was to become the terminus, and around the terminus would grow the mighty city of Vancouver. When he first saw it, there was nothing there but giant fir trees down to the shoreline, wheeling seabirds overhead and peaks already crested with snow.

They cruised like lords through the Gulf Islands, and when they arrived in Victoria, the province's capital, a banquet was held in their honour and interviews were accorded the *Times Colonist*. The Victoria of 1872 was an unruly polyglot port town of five thousand people. As Grant toured the downtown, he was amazed to see Greek fishermen, Kanaka sailors from Hawaii, Jewish and Scottish storekeepers, Chinese washerwomen, French, German and Yankee restaurateurs, black waiters and sweeps, and Australian farmers all jostling each other in the streets.

On October 14, 1872, the party said their farewells and boarded a steamer bound for San Francisco, and, five days later, climbed on board the Union Pacific, heading for Chicago and home. At the dusty little railway stations in Nevada and Utah, Grant noticed that the sheriffs had posted Wanted posters with rewards for the capture of local desperadoes. This confirmed in him the contrast between the lawless American West and the peace, order and good government that generally prevailed back home. From Chicago to Toronto, then to Ottawa and finally to Halifax, Grant reached home on November 1, 1872. His long-suffering wife, Jessie, was nine months pregnant, and within days their first child, my grandfather William Lawson Grant, was born.

Three weeks after his return, Grant gave his first lecture to a Halifax audience on the West and its future. *Ocean to Ocean: Sandford Fleming's Expedition Through*

Canada in 1872 was published the next year, and a further edition followed in 1877, with a frontispiece depicting Grant in a clergyman's homburg and Fleming in a kepi, seated in the middle of a canoe, while the Metis and Iroquois steersmen shot the rapids. The book remained in print throughout Grant's life. He had found his calling: the promotion of a national dream.

II

Grant and Fleming returned brimming with confidence that their dream would be quickly realized. The Americans had completed their railway in four years, and they were certain Canada could do it in the same time or less. In fact, thirteen long years were to elapse before the last spike was hammered in at Craigellachie. Provincial publics soured on the project, progress through the muskeg of northern Ontario was achingly slow, the costs escalated beyond the reach of a small, struggling Dominion and governments kept losing their nerve. Worst of all, from Fleming's point of view, his advice was ignored. The Yellowhead route was discarded in favour of a southern pass.

In 1877, Grant left Halifax and St. Matthew's and accepted the principalship of Queen's in Kingston, at that time a Presbyterian college on the brink of financial ruin. He saw an opportunity to give a new country a university of world quality. He took Queen's by the scruff of the neck and doggedly remade it in the image of the universities he knew from Scotland and Europe, luring professors from overseas and persuading Fleming to become the chair of the Board of Governors.

In September 1883, Fleming, now on the board of the CPR, went west to see how the work was progressing and Grant went with him. This time, they wanted to be the first Canadians to cross Canada by the pass through British Columbia's Kicking Horse River valley, the new route discovered by the American railway engineer Major A.B. Rogers. By then, the railway ran to Calgary, and so the journey that eleven years earlier had taken them two months now took a matter of days. Fleming and Grant were disillusioned by what they saw as they journeyed west: the frenzied land speculation, the disintegration of the Western Cree, now reduced to begging at the railway stations, and the toxic resentment of the railway company by the farmers and merchants forced to pay the railway's monopoly prices for freight.

They missed the joys of the old days, bursting into full gallop on the plains, like schoolboys out for a holiday run, camping at night under the stars and waking the next morning to the Metis cry *"Leve! Leve!"*

In Calgary they saddled up pack horses and a team and set off into the Bow Valley, happy to be out on the trail again with wranglers and horsemen and cowboys. But they were getting a bit old to be playing this game, a university president and a railroad tycoon well into their middle age, and they discovered that the trail up to the Rogers Pass was as tough as anything they had encountered on their earlier trip. The trail was dizzyingly steep, unstable underfoot and encumbered with deadfall. The two men had to muster all their determination to get to the top. Finally, one September afternoon, aching, bruised and dirty, they blundered their way to the summit and found Major Rogers and his survey party awaiting them.

A grand afternoon ensued. A picnic was spread out on the grass. Grant said some prayers, and even Rogers, a famously coarse and hard-driving sinner, bowed his head. Afterward, Fleming broke out Havana cigars and everyone had a celebratory smoke for the occasion, all envisaging the day when the railway would come through the pass and link the provinces into a single nation. As the light began to fade that September afternoon, the festivities concluded with the improbable spectacle of Grant and Fleming, two grand adolescents, playing leapfrog in the meadow, while Major Rogers looked on, smoking his cigar.

Two years later, Fleming journeyed out west again, this time in the company of Donald Smith. The train took them through the Kicking Horse Pass to a ceremony that marked the conclusion of the whole great adventure. Grant doesn't figure in the famous photograph of the driving in of the last spike—it is dominated by a top-hatted Fleming and Smith—but he was there in spirit. Even the name that Fleming and Smith chose for the place where that spike was driven had special meaning for a Grant. The name they chose—Craigellachie—happened to be the ancestral home of the Grant clan, and every Grant knew the war cry "Stand Fast, Craigellachie!"

The railway secured Canada's continental future and guaranteed that the West would not be absorbed by the Americans. Yet Grant knew by then that all national dreams, all acts of nation building, at least in Canada, are achieved at someone's expense. The railway destroyed a rival way of life. By 1885, the Plains Cree were on reservations. The railway was used to ferry troops to put down Riel's second rebellion, the last stand of the Metis, French and Aboriginal way of life built on the buffalo hunt and the fur trade. Riel stood trial in Regina that year. The country was bitterly divided over Riel's fate, with Orangemen in Ontario calling for blood and Quebec demanding a pardon. Grant thought Riel a poor deluded fool and called publicly for pardon. Prime Minister Macdonald bowed to Ontario. Riel went to the gallows, and a martyr, for both the Metis nation and for Quebec, was born.

Riel's execution caused fury throughout Quebec. The rising star of the Liberal Party, Wilfrid Laurier, took the stage at a rally in Montreal in November 1885, shortly after the execution, and defended Riel in vehement terms, saying that had he himself been on the banks of the Saskatchewan, he, too, would have taken up a musket against the troops. Protestant Ontario never allowed him to forget those words.

The achievement of Grant's dream, therefore, drove fissures through the fabric of Canada that remain to this day. Quebec's leading figures believed that the railway had been used to destroy French society in the West.

In 1890, when the government of Manitoba went so far as to abolish the separate Roman Catholic school system and replace it with a single "national" board, Quebec's worst fears were confirmed, and for six years, the federation was convulsed by a crisis at once religious, educational and national in character.

The Manitoba schools crisis grieved Grant—the worst civil war, he wrote, is that in which "a church is arrayed against the state." In September 1895, by now pushing sixty, he took a month away from his duties as university president and went to Manitoba, patiently reporting from both sides of the dispute for the Toronto *Globe*.

His reports strongly condemned the Manitoba government for shutting down the French school system, remarking tartly that there was no need to burn a house down in order to taste crackling. Already Winnipeg schools were crowded with the new immigrants flooding into the West—Norwegians, Icelanders, Germans, Jews, Ukrainians—but the Franco-Manitobans were staying away, attending their own underfunded private schools rather than submit to Protestant instruction in English. Grant understood and accepted their refusal. He came away believing that national unity did not require a single national school system; confessional education in two languages was a necessity in a country as divided as Canada. What the nation needed was more bilingual education, so that citizens grew up comfortable in both official languages and comfortable with the religious opinions of their neighbours. Nor did he favour the use of federal power to compel national standards. He did not believe the federal government had the right to disallow the provincial schools legislation; instead, he urged the province to think again and provide public support for French Catholic education.

He had learned an important lesson from those hours on the trail with the French Metis, from those days spent patiently listening to aggrieved French schoolteachers in small schoolrooms in St. Boniface. He wrote that the alluring vision of a homogeneous and united people sometimes tempts Canadians, but they must never forget "that a people can be truly united only when great minorities do not feel themselves treated with injustice."

III

The railway forged Canada's identity as a nation from ocean to ocean, but the national vision was linked, in Grant's and Fleming's minds, to a still grander imperial design. The transcontinental shortened the distance between London and the Antipodes. It drew the global empire closer together and increased Canada's importance as a global spoke in the imperial hub. The CPR quickly became a worldwide transportation company, with grand hotels at every terminus, from the Château Frontenac in Quebec to the Empress in Victoria, and steamships travelling from Vancouver to Sydney, Australia, to Yokahama, Japan, and to Calcutta, India.

For Grant this was the grander destiny that made the slog up to the Rogers Pass worthwhile, the vision that made him persevere back home among the doubters and doomsayers, the scornful homebodies whose horizon was the parish pump or the province. Canada itself was always a dream for him, never just a reality. It achieved grandeur in his mind when it took its place in a larger design.

These conceptions were no abstraction. He was a man who lived ideals to the full. He never had a vision but set out immediately to experience it in practice. In 1887, worn out by a decade of work at Queen's, he was rewarded with a sabbatical, and he took it in a typically ambitious form: a world tour of the British Empire.

The tour took him to Scotland, of course, but also to his home away from home, the Colonial Institute on Northumberland Avenue near Trafalgar Square in London. There he met all the worthies who believed in imperial federation, the ruling idea of the last decades of his life. The federation he sought would leave the dominions in full possession of their domestic independence and sovereignty and, in addition, would give Canada a stronger voice in world affairs because it would have a seat at a federal imperial parliament with jurisdiction over foreign affairs, defence and transportation. Grant was by then a sufficiently senior propagandist in this cause to gain the confidence of British politicians such as Joseph Chamberlain, who were then promoting imperial federation in the British Parliament.

The empire for Grant was both a cause and the most exclusive club to which a provincial Canadian could ever belong. As he prepared to sail for Cape Town, he collected letters of introduction from the leaders of the imperialist cause to their counterparts in the other British colonies. Shipowners gave him free passage around the world on their steamers, so great was the prestige then associated with his cause. Everyone received him, including the greatest living custodian of the English language itself, Dr. James Murray, directing the compilation of the first edition of the *Oxford English Dictionary*, in a scriptorium—a greenhouse-like shed—constructed in the back garden of his Oxford house.

Murray sought Grant's assistance with Canadian terms and idioms, though we do not learn what they were.

Globalization was well underway in Grant's time. Letters from Kingston, Ontario, could reach London, England, in two weeks. Grant could tell his wife to write him care of the governor of the Cape Colony in South Africa and expect to have the letters awaiting his arrival, three weeks later. The ship that took him south of the equator was carrying frozen New Zealand carcasses of lamb. Sandford Fleming was organizing a global time system, based on the Greenwich meridian, to bring coherence to railway timetables, ship sailings and all the other activities that needed to be coordinated through standard time in a global economy. The leading technologies of the day—such as Alexander Graham Bell's telephone, then just entering commercial application—were already pointing the way to undersea cables, and Fleming was already envisaging their use as a way to link the empire in instantaneous communication. This was globalization with a very reassuring face, not under the sovereignty of a market, with a centre everywhere and nowhere, obeying no laws but its own, but a globalization under the sovereignty of a queen, a flag and a navy, a globalization advancing under the language of Shakespeare and under the benediction of a Protestant God.

If other empires were then joining in the scramble for resources and possessions, if Britain was actually fast approaching imperial twilight, nothing gave George Grant any sign of this. As he travelled into the southern latitudes, dining at the captain's table, conducting Sunday service for passengers in the lounge, pacing the decks at night, with the stars above and the ship rolling beneath his feet, he wrote home to Jessie and confessed, a little shamefacedly, that he had never felt so well in his life.

The trip was a stupendous adventure encompassing South Africa, Tasmania, Australia, New Zealand, Japan, the Philippines and then Canada, where he travelled from Vancouver home to Kingston via his beloved railway. But one stop in particular, South Africa, turned out to be signally important, both to the fate of the empire and to his conception of it.

He had introductions to the governor of the province and all the local dignitaries, and while he was there he visited the vineyards of Stellenbosch, the diamond mines of Kimberley, mulatto churches and Christian missions, and witnessed the sounding fury of the ocean beating on the southernmost rocks of Africa. Everywhere he went he compared what he saw to Canada, the veldt so burnt and bare, like the Prairies in high summer. It was both the same—a British colonial society—and different—a kingdom built upon a brutal racial hierarchy. In the De Beers diamond mine, he peered into a walled enclosure at the mine entrance where the black workers were corralled, forbidden to return to their homes in the bush until they had finished their contracts. There were more than two thousand "niggers"—he used the term in quotation marks—resting, sleeping, talking, laughing, some in groups preparing their supper, others at a short religious service, still others lighting fires and playing cards. They were indentured slaves, in effect, who on expiry of their contracts would return to tribal homelands and their wives and children. This was the other side of empire, the infernal labour, the primitive accumulation, that made all the high-minded dreams possible.

Grant recoiled at the outright racial hatred of the Boers for the black majority. He wrote home to Jessie to tell her that one of the Boers had taken him aside and recounted in shocked tones that in the nearby Portuguese colony of Mozambique, Portuguese actually married coloured people. We have never sunk so low, the Boer told him.

On the train back from the mines, he shared a carriage with a Mr. Botha, member of the colonial Upper House and president of the Afrikaner Bond, a Boer organization seeking to establish Dutch supremacy in South Africa. Botha, Grant thought, was exactly like a Presbyterian elder in some rural county in the Maritimes, a man, he perceptively added, "to be led not driven." Grant thought their racial prejudices unchristian, but he could not help admiring men like Botha, industrious, ascetic and severe Christians like himself, so fiercely committed to freedom, as they conceived it, that when the British liberated the slaves and ended the slave trade in the 1840s, they trekked north to found their own homeland in the Transvaal.

The Boer Wars between 1898 and 1902 were the most serious crisis to befall the British Empire since the loss of the American colonies in 1783. By 1898 Grant was in his sixties, plagued by kidney trouble, exhausted by university administration and visibly aging, drawn and white-whiskered in the photographs. His wife, Jessie, was also failing, having never fully recovered from the loss of their beloved son Geordie.

The crisis in South Africa taxed Grant further, because it pulled apart two elements—the imperial and the national—that he had managed to reconcile for most of his life. Canada, he believed, had succeded in bringing together these opposing ideals. In the completion of its national dream, it had strengthened both its independence from and its ties to the imperial mother. In the Boer rebellion, the national and the imperial had split apart. A child of empire was demanding complete independence.

Grant's sympathies with the Boers ran deep, because he was more than sensitive to the imperial injustice and rapacity that had provoked them into revolt. Cecil Rhodes, the British adventurer whose raid on the Transvaal had provoked the second Boer uprising, was, in Grant's eyes, nothing more than a pirate in top hat and patent leather boots. "I hope to see the rascal hanged," he confided angrily. As for the Boers, he saw in them the image of the hardy settlers who were peopling the empty Prairies of Canada.

The Boer struggle triggered deeper doubts about Canada's own position in the empire. "We govern ourselves, yet are not independent," he wrote. "We assert that we are now not simply a colony or dependency, but we are unable to define what we really are." We have few independent thinkers, he conceded, and are accustomed to taking our opinions on most subjects from England.

Grant fumed at the "patronizing language too often used by British newspapers," and he railed at the "inconsistent language of politicians of the Manchester school who with one breath declare the colonies useless to the empire, and with the next express amazement that they should presume to understand their own business." It was galling to love an empire that did not love you back.

Worst of all, he admitted, Canada could be plunged into war at any time, "without our having a word to say as to the why." In 1898, this moment of truth arrived: The empire was insisting that as long as Britain was at war with the Boers, so was Canada. What was Canada to do?

Canada had been asked to provide a contingent to assist Britain in putting down the rebellion, and Grant's old friend Donald Smith, now Lord Strathcona, living in state on Montreal's Sherbrooke Street, had offered to assemble, at his own expense, a cavalry regiment of Canadian volunteers to fight for queen and empire.

Until mid-1899, Grant sided with the Boers, opposing a British invasion of the Transvaal, but when the Boers issued an ultimatum in September 1899 ordering the British to remove their troops from the Transvaal border, Grant's position cracked. He could not stand with renegades when imperial order was defied. When the Boers moved against British possessions in South Africa, "there was nothing to do but fight it out to a finish."

Canada, he believed, must answer the imperial call. "We aspire to be a nation, and how can we realize that high ideal save by doing the work and submitting to the sacrifices demanded by national life?" He supported the dispatch of Lord Strathcona's Light Horse contingent and, in letters to Laurier, strongly counselled a much more reluctant prime minister that Parliament should shoulder the expense of a Canadian detachment.

By now the old man was entering his final years alone. His beloved wife had died, his remaining son was teaching in Toronto and his flagging energies were devoted to defending the empire's unity in its hour of need. The South African war was supposed to be a quick and glorious fight, but it soon turned into a bitter and costly struggle. Quebec refused to support the imperial venture, and the war soon widened existing national divisions. Laurier found himself defied within his own party by Henri Bourassa.

In his last public address, delivered on January 6, 1902, in a quavering voice, Grant appealed to Quebeckers, saying he understood why they wouldn't want to fight for an English king in a faraway land. But he reserved his bitterest irony for those, including Laurier, who opposed the idea of Canada contributing to the cost of imperial defence:

> We give the bravest of our children to die by the bullet or still deadlier disease; but some one else must pay their wages. We do not grudge the blood of our sons, but with a treasury so full … we grudge food, clothing and transport for them. Let Canada accept the blood money without a blush. This state of things cannot continue. The empire must be practically as well as nominally united.

Unity of nation and empire, unity of one *through* the consolidation of the other: this had been his life's vision, and he stood by it to his last breath, as Canadian soldiers were cut down in the velds and kopjes of a faraway country, as the British herded the Boers into their new invention, the concentration camp, and thousands died of disease and starvation. I do not know whether my great-grandfather knew, at the end, that the empire had come to this, because in May 1902, as the war dragged into its third year, he died in his sleep, at the age of sixty-seven.

3
AFTER THE SOMME

William Grant was at his father's bedside in those final days. He heard the old man whisper, "Give me a chance; Oh my God, give me a chance." Then later, the son heard the father, his eyes shut, imploring, "Get it done, get it done quickly." After days of growing weaker, he whispered "Jessie"—his wife's name—and then slipped into unconsciousness.

On May 13, 1902, there was a funeral service at Convocation Hall at Queen's, and afterward a procession of the coffin through the streets of Kingston. William followed the coffin to its final resting place, noting that the crowd lining the streets was as large as the one that had come out for the funeral of Kingston's other favourite son, Sir John A. Macdonald. Late that afternoon, George Monro Grant was laid to rest in Cataraqui Cemetery, next to his wife and his son Geordie.

The death of parents always unleashes paradoxical emotions: grief, guilt, relief and liberation all at once. We can only infer which of these was strongest. The son could step out of his father's shadow, yet the shadow had given his life shape and meaning. Moreover, he was now alone. He was a schoolmaster at Upper Canada College and, as he looked to the future, he saw before him a solitary life of teaching and scholarship. As for marriage, he did not think himself much of a catch: small in stature, wiry and balding, a sedentary and unadventurous bachelor approaching middle age. It is not that women had not caught his eye. From afar, he had admired Maude Parkin, the daughter of his principal at Upper Canada, George Parkin. In 1902 Parkin left for England to set up the Rhodes Scholarships and Maude left with her family. After the Parkins departed, William left UCC too, taking up another job as a schoolmaster at St. Andrew's College near Toronto.

For the next two years, he wrote a scholarly biography of his father, Victorian in length and in piety. *Principal Grant* registers admiration, love and astonishment at the energy, briskness and drive of his father. He had truly been a "steam engine in trousers," as one of the old man's friends used to say. Poring over his father's diaries and letters gave the son a last chance to stay close, but once the biography was published, we can imagine the silence that flowed into his life.

Fifteen years later, he admitted that he continued to see his father "so vividly that I am not yet fully sure in my own mind whether it was dream or vision, or resurrection if you call it so."

His father was gone but his father's causes remained his own. He believed his vocation now was to teach bright young men to lead lives devoted to public service in Canada and the empire. One of these young men at St. Andrew's College was Vincent Massey, heir to the Massey-Harris tractor fortune. Truth was, Grant was soon restless at St. Andrew's College, teaching worthy sentiments to the rich young sons of the Ontario business elite.

After his biography of his father appeared in 1904, he took himself off to France and lived in Paris for two years. There he researched and wrote the life of Samuel de Champlain, founder of Quebec and New France, and mastered French and took classes at the Sorbonne. He loved Paris and even a decade later could still remember the names of the tastiest dishes in his favourite *brasseries*. He remained a committed francophile for the rest of his life. Living in France seems to have changed his view of the country back home, for among historians of his generation, he was unusual in his interest in the contribution of France to the making of his country. He spent several years editing Lescarbot's *Histoire de la Nouvelle France* for publication in English. When he wrote his *History of Canada* for the secondary schools of Ontario, many English-speaking

Canadians found it strange that he should attach equal importance to the French fact in the making of Canadian distinctiveness. British Columbia school districts refused to use the book because of its francophile bias.

He was ambitious and hoped, for a time, he would become famous. For a Canadian of his generation, fame meant success in England, and when a chance for academic advancement offered itself, he took it. Alfred Beit, a business partner of Cecil Rhodes in South Africa, endowed a lectureship at Oxford and Grant put his name forward. He had reason to be hopeful. In 1894, he had been the first Canadian to win a first-class degree in classics at Oxford. In 1906, he was named the first Beit Lecturer in Colonial History and quickly settled back into life in his old college, Balliol. He proved to be a productive scholar, completing worthy tomes on Canadian constitutional development and an edited volume of the *Acts of the Privy Council, Colonial Series*. Scholarly pursuits had some appeal to him. He was a shy man by nature, convivial in company, but never happier than when reading. He was also shrewd enough to realize that while he might lack his father's self-confidence, he surpassed him in scholarship.

He would make his own mark as a scholar, but he was too full of life to be satisfied with the musty joys of the Colonial Office archives. He once said there were few sights more joyless than a library full of scholars buried in forgotten tomes. Boring academic papers could rouse him to scathing acts of mimicry. He was a scholar all right, but a restless one.

At Oxford, an unusual experiment in education was just then starting—the Workers' Educational Association, or WEA, an alliance between labour and the universities to provide tutorial classes for working-class adults. Grant went to the meetings at Ruskin College and became an enthusiastic tutor for the WEA. Later in life, he was to become a founder of the WEA in Canada, as well as a supporter of Frontier College, a pioneering initiative to take university education to the logging camps and mining sites of northern Ontario. There was a certain *noblesse oblige* in this idea of university men teaching the working classes, but there was something admirable in the idea, too. He really did believe the class divisions of an industrial country could be healed by good teaching.

Being Beit Lecturer offered Grant a further means of escape into a wider and more influential world, since it brought him into contact with the leading British imperial figures of his day. The colonial governor of South Africa, Lord Milner, was now back in Britain, assembling around him a group of bright young imperialists known as the Milner Kindergarten. Grant delivered academic papers with Milner in the chair and befriended Milner's intense acolyte Lionel Curtis, a Boer War veteran turned imperialist intellectual.

The Boer Wars left unclear what duties the dominions owed the mother country in a European conflict. Lionel Curtis pressed this issue especially hard. Were the dominions—South Africa, Canada, Australia and New Zealand—sovereign over issues of peace and war? If they were truly sovereign, would they come to the aid of the mother country if she were attacked by Germany? If they were not sovereign, would they be automatically at war if Germany attacked? Curtis and Milner created the Round Table, an informal circle of bright young men from around the empire, to hammer out an answer. Grant took part in these debates but refused to be drawn in too far, arguing that Canada couldn't make commitments until the threat from Germany and other states materialized.

One of the places where these questions were discussed was an imposing three-storey brick house modestly called the Cottage, in Goring-on-Thames, near Oxford. This was the home of George R. Parkin, now secretary of the Rhodes Trust. An elegant, handsome, supremely self-confident, pious Victorian always photographed in a wing collar and frock coat, Parkin was the most influential living exponent of imperial federation and was such a devoted admirer of William Grant's father that he kept a photograph of George Monro Grant hanging on the wall of his study. Despite their mutual admiration, the contrast between Parkin and Grant was interesting. Grant remained the doughty, persevering Scottish Canadian, while Parkin had passed himself off as more British than the British. William took a respectful but ironic view of Parkin, once remarking that "I don't think he got God and Oxford and the British Empire wholly separated."

The Grants' vision of empire was less romantic than Parkin's. While the Grants thought Cecil Rhodes was a rascal, George Parkin was carrying out the old rascal's dying wish to create a scholarship that would create a new English-speaking elite among the empires of the day.

Nobody meeting the very British Parkin could have guessed that he had begun life amidst the farms and lumber mill towns of New Brunswick's St. John River valley. He had started out as a rural schoolmaster and had managed, by sheer force of personality, to get himself to Oxford in the early 1870s. There he astonished audiences at Union Debates with his vision of the British Empire as the bearer of Christian civilization to the lesser breeds. Alfred Milner attributed his dedication to the imperialist cause to the impact of the young Parkin. After his miraculous year at Oxford, Parkin returned to schoolmastering in New Brunswick, but he had made such a vivid impression that when the Imperial Federation League was looking for a spokesman, they sought out the tall and impressive young man from New Brunswick. Through the late 1880s and early 1890s, he became the movement's chief representative, travelling to Australia and New Zealand and across Canada preaching that the dominions should seek representation in the imperial parliament in London. In this way, they could affirm their national identity and their imperial destiny.

Parkin was a master of the podium, but he did not convince every audience. Imperial federation proved controversial in the Antipodes. Most Australians and New Zealanders didn't like the idea that their citizens might be taxed and sent to die in imperial wars. Imperial federation drew a warmer hearing in Canada because of the threatening proximity of the United States. Parkin, like Grant, felt certain that Canada could not survive unless the British connection was paramount in Canadian national life.

For William Grant the Cottage at Goring-on-Thames would have felt like the old family house in Kingston, if on a grander scale: carpeted with Afghan and Persian rugs, the shelves of the study library crammed with history, philosophy and theology, the drawing rooms filled with the sounds of piano, all available surfaces crowded with the African knickknacks the *paterfamilias* had brought back from his travels. On becoming secretary of the Rhodes Trust, Parkin had journeyed to southern Africa to visit Rhodes's grave. At some dusty roadside stand, he brought as presents for his daughters, Maude, Alice and Marjorie, and his son, Raleigh, a set of wooden carvings of a wildebeest, an ostrich, a leopard, a hippo and a giraffe. These endearing carvings were to follow the Parkin children and their descendants through every twist and turn of their lives.

In 1909 and 1910, William returned again and again to Goring to enjoy the company of the Parkin girls, especially Maude. She was six years his junior, a vivacious and accomplished blue-stocking. She had graduated from McGill, still a relatively rare achievement for a woman of her time, and, after following her father to England, was serving as a warden at a woman's residence at the University of Manchester. In the photographs of her as a young woman, with hair piled up on top of her head and prim white blouse buttoned up to the neck, the striking features are her thin pursed lips and the set jaw. She was a thoughtful, earnest young woman, but also stylish, refined and full of life. At Manchester, she impressed many with her organizational abilities and skill with undergraduates. One of her friendships was with a young chemist, Chaim Weizmann, just then beginning his career as a leader of British Zionism. Maude Parkin made a sufficiently vivid impression on Weizmann that, forty years later, when he was president of Israel, he still remembered his old Manchester colleague.

At the end of each Manchester term, Maude would return to Goring, and there, as often as not, she would find herself sometimes alone in the salon, sometimes in the gardens, with William Grant. She would have noted that her father, on whom she doted, thought him a clever and coming man. But she would have had little idea of William's feelings for her, for they were all bottled up inside.

By the summer of 1910, Grant had been lured home to Canada by an offer of an endowed chair in colonial and Canadian history at Queen's. He had been away six years. If he remained in England, he knew that he would never be accepted as one of the tribe. Parkin had done well passing as an Englishman, but Grant lacked his graces and political finesse. If Grant went home to Queen's, he reckoned, life might be more provincial, but he knew he belonged there.

It was not until early August 1910, with departure for Canada only a month away, that he screwed up his courage and wrote "Miss Maude" a letter in which he declared his true feelings. He admitted that he had always seen himself as a confirmed bachelor, but their last few months together had changed his plans for life. He confessed that he was old, pushing forty, but hoped there was still the play of life in him yet. He burst out finally: "I have come to love you very deeply. There! It is said now, and nothing else makes much difference."

He told her that with her at his side "we can do ten times as much for Canada" as he could do alone, and then, realizing she might think he wanted her just for what she could bring to his work, he blurted out: "My dear, whenever I think of you, when I speak your name, the pulses in my neck quiver and tighten, and all my blood seems to be in my throat."

It was a touching letter and it did the trick. Within a week, they met in London, Maude accepted him, Mr. and Mrs. Parkin gave their approval and the engagement was announced.

It is worth pausing over the phrase in William Grant's declaration about working together for Canada. Commit to help each other, commit to stay with each other in sickness and in health, certainly, but commit to Canada? Yet it was not just a fine phrase, but central to Grant's sense of what his life—and hers—were for.

By mid-September 1910, he was on his way across the Atlantic, back to Kingston, and she back to Manchester. Letters, sometimes two a day, would pass back and forth between them. He confessed, "I am not a great man. I have read their biographies and they all write to their lady loves as if they were addressing a large and highly culti-vated Public Meeting … whereas I write to you about You and Me."

Sometimes, as the days passed and a letter would not come, he would break into a kind of half-comic despair:

Will you always love me? Always? In the commonplace days? If my hair falls out? If the maid gives warning and we have to cook our own dinner? If I make a bad speech? And my class despise my lectures? If all goes wrong? When you are overworked, and we have to take a second best holiday because we can't afford the one we want? Will you always love me?

As 1910 turned into 1911, she wanted to know what position he took on the issue of trade reciprocity, the great question dividing the country. Laurier went into the elections with a proposal to lower tariffs on all American goods. The Conservatives opposed, believing that reciprocity would jeopardize Canadian manufacturers, weaken the British connection and threaten the identity of the country. Maude's father was almost certainly with the Conservatives on this issue. Grant sided with Laurier and the Liberals but added, pointedly, that "we prate of our Canadian nationalism … yet we have so little real confidence in our nationality that a large part of us think it likely to founder if the US take off their tariff on a few of our natural products. A somewhat precarious nationalism, surely!"

In the election of 1911, Robert Borden became prime minister, and Laurier was swept from office on fears in English Canada that continental integration with the Americans would weaken Canada and on suspicions in Quebec that Laurier had wanted to tie the country too closely to the British Empire.

Over the seven months that Maude and William were apart, from September 1910 to April 1911, they slowly revealed their secrets to each other. She wrote to him a solemn letter about her ideals and about the "need for grace and refinement and restraint as well as strength," and he agreed but told her that these were very hard ideals to realize in Canada, where "the tendency is all slap-dash hustle." He jokingly called her "my little Puritan," but he knew he was one too. They were both faithful church-goers, yet something was changing inside him, taking him away from the faith of his father. He confessed to her, "I rarely, terribly rarely now feel the need of Divine Aid or Communion. I want to work for my fellows, to be in com-munion with them, but God comes terribly little into my thoughts and I fear Christ even less."

The simple truth may have been that he was discov-ering, in those solitary months alone, grading student papers, eating a lonely meal at the local Chinese restaurant in Kingston, waiting for her letters to come, pouring out his heart to her, that love and desire mattered more to him than faith.

They were finally married in June 1911 in the parish church at Goring-on-Thames, she in a high-necked white lace dress with a train, he in a wing-necked collar and tail coat. In their wedding pictures, they look happy and a little frightened.

After a honeymoon in northern Italy, they returned to Kingston in the autumn of 1911. In the three years that followed, he shared the grumbling that Queen's was not what it had been in his father's day, but he was also proud that Queen's mattered mightily in the Dominion. With his colleagues O.D. Skelton and Adam Shortt, he set about training the men who created Canada's first fully professional civil service in Ottawa. At home, he discovered in himself a love of family life he never expected. He shouted his happiness from the rooftops, telling one of his friends that "the desire of men for women is heaven born."

As for Maude Grant, there is little doubt that she loved him and flowered in domestic intimacy, but Kingston was no match for Goring and her new life was more confining than the old. She had enjoyed professional respect at the University of Manchester. Now she was the dutiful wife of Principal Grant's son, having to make conversation with every Kingston matron who remembered the grand old man and who had an opinion about the less spectacular son. Soon she was pregnant, and within three years, she had two infant daughters, Margaret and Charity, to care for. She was in her mid-thirties when the children were born, and, although the births went well, her life was swallowed up by domestic chores.

The summer of 1914 found the family in England, she with the children at her parents' house at Goring, he in London, working at the Royal Colonial Institute on a biography of his father's idol, Joseph Howe, colonial orator and the first man to achieve responsible government for a British colony.

When the European crisis broke out with the assassination of the archduke in Sarajevo and the subsequent Austrian ultimatum to Serbia on July 28, 1914, Grant was putting the finishing touches on his biography of Howe. As the European powers rushed to war, Grant put away his books and went down to the House of Commons to listen to the speeches. In a letter to Maude at Goring, he confessed that the political situation "grips me, overwhelms me." The prospect of war put him, he said, "in the same state that I was in when, in the hope of keeping my independence, I fought against telling you of my love and was at last swept away." The war fever gripping the capital had seized hold of him, too.

He stopped going to the archives and joined the crowds in Trafalgar Square and Whitehall. He anxiously discussed the situation with a friend, Maurice Hankey, soon to become secretary to the War Cabinet. With his father-in-law, George Parkin, one August afternoon, he walked through the streets, noticing the broken windows at the German embassy and the frenetic excitement of the crowds. On Whitehall, they noticed that the National Union of Women's Suffrage had set up a stand and was enlisting women for war work. Sentries were posted at Charing Cross Railway Station. He and Parkin bumped into Lord Sydenham, who told them that Parliament had adjourned. Parkin and Grant elbowed their way down Pall Mall to Buckingham Palace, until they were right in front of the iron gates amid the clamouring crowd. As he reported to Maude that night,

> Just then out came the King, Queen and Prince on the balcony. We cheered and waved and they waved and bowed standing for about 5 minutes. Pandemonium; some cheering, some singing God Save the King, others Rule Britannia!

His first thought was to enlist. He had already, while a master at Upper Canada, done service in a reserve regiment, so he was officer material, but his chief worry was that at forty-two years of age, he might be judged too old for active duty. At Canada House, he was told to get back to Canada and enlist there.

Few Canadians would have been as susceptible to the drum beat of martial patriotism as William Grant. He believed in the cause of empire; he thought of citizenship as service and sacrifice; and now at last the empire had sounded the call to arms. In a letter to Maude written in August 1914, William said that looking into his own heart was like peering through smoked glass into the white heat of a furnace. Inside him, he admitted, he could feel the "fierce, hellish spirit of this war."

But what could a forty-two-year-old professor contribute to the war effort? While waiting to return to Canada, he persuaded the Royal Colonial Institute and

Heinemann Publishers to let him produce a short pamphlet on the causes of the war. In late August and early September, as German armies poured into Belgium and the French struggled to hold them at the Marne, Grant immersed himself in the works of the key ideologists of German expansion, von Treitschke and von Bernhardi, Kaiser Wilhelm and Prince von Bulow. Grant's idea was to provide the general public, especially the enlisted soldier, with a pocket compendium of quotations that would illustrate the righteousness of the cause. Grant set out to convict German militarism, using only its own words. In the final pages of *Our Just Cause,* he argued that the Allies were at war because of the "swelled head" of the German militarist classes, because of "our plighted word to France and Belgium" and "in the cause of civilization and of liberty and of international law." In the final paragraph, written as news of German atrocities in Belgium were filling the British and French press, he concluded that the empire must fight to the finish to avenge Belgium, to extirpate Prussian militarism and, finally, "to vindicate our character as a fighting race."

A fighting race. Just two years before, Grant might have shrunk from such language. Now it came naturally. *Our Just Cause* was a stirring, if bellicose, performance from a scholar. It was successful enough to go through at least two editions.

The question that he and so many Canadians had debated in those years of peace—whether if Britain were at war, Canada would be at war as well—was now moot. The empire had called. Canada—proud member of the fighting race—could only answer yes. It never occurred to Grant to think otherwise.

Neither Maude nor William doubted that she should stay in England with her parents and that he should return as soon as he could to enlist in Canada. Raleigh, Maude's teenage brother, immediately enlisted and the Cottage was busy with sending him off. Goring, it should be noted, was near the southeast coast of England and, by the autumn of 1914, it was not hard to imagine that one could hear the distant thunder of the guns on the battlefields of France across the Channel.

Finally, William returned to Canada. From late 1914 through the winter of 1916, he trained in Gananoque and other Canadian army camps, writing Maude sometimes twice and three times a day, letters that he used as a diary of the grinding routine of camp life: route marches, parade drills, weapons inspections, delousing details, censorship of recruits' letters and court martial sessions for violations of discipline, mostly drunken escapades in the local towns. He missed Maude and the children, and sometimes a note of raw sexual longing enters the correspondence. He managed a leave early in the summer of 1915 and visited them all in Goring, and the encounter revived their physical passion for each other. In February 1916, Maude proudly announced the arrival of Jessie Alison Grant, their third daughter. Maude was worried that William would have wanted a boy, and William admitted that he might have preferred it, hastening to add, "just for the variety, no feelings whatever about the superior sex."

In the muddy, often frozen training camps at Gananoque, he discovered a capacity for leadership he had not suspected. He joked that army life was not supposed to suit an old professor, but he was used to motivating young men half his age. He told Maude, rather proudly, that they called him Daddy. When his contingents were ready to be shipped off to France, he was there waving at the platform at Gananoque station, choked up to see them heading off to battle and to God knew what prospects of survival.

> And so they went, drunk and sober, rough necks and gentlemen—and how many of them shall I see again? One loves one's men, the rougher they are, the simpler they are, the more one loves them. We started Auld Lang Syne but after about a line and a half, Daddy Grant had to stop and turn away.

By early 1916, the Canadian newspapers carried columns of the names of the dead. His classmates at Queen's were dying. Balliol College sent him the lists of the college men who had been lost and his heart tightened to see how many of them, the bright sparks of the 1890s, were no more. The boys he had taught at Upper Canada and at St. Andrew's were also falling. He went on recruitment drives to the small towns of eastern Ontario and noticed, with fury and resignation, that the boys were no longer coming forward to serve. He wrote Maude,

> We have almost reached the limits of the voluntary system even with the high pay and other inducements which we offer. The native-born Canadian especially in the small country village is very slack and when he does come forward, his woman kind do all they can to dissuade him.

The British born had come forward, but not the immigrants and the native-born Canadians. As the carnage continued, as the waste of young life carried on, month after month, the cause that was sacred to him ceased to be sacred for millions of Canadians. The spectre of conscription brought these divisions out into the open. Laurier and the Liberals supported the war but opposed conscription, knowing that while many French Canadians were fighting in France, Quebec as a whole would never accept forced participation in a war for king and country. Prime Minister Borden and his Cabinet believed conscription was necessary if Canada was to keep its pledge to the empire.

Through 1916 and 1917, William Grant lived through a moment of truth about the Canadian identity that his father would never have imagined possible. The Grants—and the Parkins—believed that loyalty to empire was at the core of being Canadian. The war in Europe now pulled the braided strands of loyalty to country and empire apart. French Canada simply did not see its identity in imperial terms. William was honest enough to acknowledge this. Ontario Orangemen might castigate the Québécois for cowardice, but Grant knew this was absurd and an evasion of the real issue: Could the empire keep demanding such sacrifice of its sons and daughters?

As for himself, whatever inner doubts began to prey, he knew his duty. When his turn came and his battalion was shipped to England for final training before dispatch to the front, he was ready to go. We shall soon be together, he told Maude, and "I shall see Miss Alison Grant," the daughter he had not yet held in his arms. On arrival in England, however, there was little home leave. Instead, his days were filled with route marching through the Hampshire lanes and with weapons training, learning how to operate the Mills bomb, the hand grenade of its time, and mastering the operation of his pistol, his trench shovel and, the most fearsome instrument of all, the gas mask.

When he came home to see the family at Goring-on-Thames, he was in the uniform of the Canadian Expeditionary Force. The whole family was on a war footing. Maude's brother, Raleigh, only eighteen, was serving at Gallipoli. He would soon be wounded and invalided home. Alice Parkin—Lal, as she was known—had returned to Canada to marry William's old pupil Vincent Massey, who was in a regiment in Toronto.

On June 1, 1916, the British launched the greatest single offensive of the war at the Somme. The thunder of the guns was heard at various places along the English coastline. In a single day, great regiments of the empire—the Newfoundland Regiment, the Ulster Regiment—were cut to pieces by German machine-gun fire or counter-barrage as they crossed no man's land. Grant made the crossing to France, landing at Le Havre in early August, headed for the St. Eloi salient in Flanders.

His first impression of France was peaceful: the women on the quays throwing loaves of bread up to the Canadian soldiers on the troopships and then holding out their aprons to catch the coins thrown down in payment. At the train stations, as the soldiers were being ferried up to the front, children ran up and down the platforms shouting *"Biscuit! Biscuit!"* At another stop, he had time to get out, stretch his legs, walk to a bookshop and buy a copy of Montesquieu's *Persian Letters*—soothing medicine for a quaking heart. In a letter to Maude, he said he could not tell her where he was exactly, because of wartime censorship—though it was near St. Eloi—but he noted in passing how close England was, just across the Channel. He wondered whether she could hear the guns. As he drew closer, he could hear the thunder and rattle, the cascades and clouds of smoke rising in the sky. The troop trains passed burned-out houses with flattened roofs, the tiles scattered along the tracks. Spotter planes droned overhead, leaving behind white plumes in the August sky. At the front itself, he caught his first glimpse of the awe-inspiring devastation of the St. Eloi craters, a lunar landscape of terrible destruction caused by artillery bombardment.

As they left the trains and approached the reserve trenches behind the main lines, he ran into old friends from Queen's or Upper Canada College or Kingston or Toronto and saw in their faces what awaited him. He heard brave men confess a shameful desire for a "blighty," some flesh wound that would allow them out of the charnel house of battle and a safe passage home. He learned that an old friend had been shot through the stomach two days before and had died in agony.

His unit, the 59th battalion of the 20th regiment of the Second Canadian Division of the Canadian Expeditionary Force, was joining men who had been fighting, on and off, since 1915. They had been gassed and had lost wave after wave of men, and hatred of the Germans had taken hold of some of the officers. The medical officer of the division, for example, wrote in his daily reports, in the sector of the front where Grant was serving, that having seen men writhing in agony after a gas attack, he believed the Canadians should take no more prisoners. "Extermination is the only remedy," he wrote.

Into this cauldron of fear and violence was thrown a sensitive, middle-aged professor, equipped with a gas mask, a pistol, a steel helmet and the determination to see it through. By day, he kept his and his men's morale going. At night, when the shelling died down and he was able to write, head down in a dugout behind sandbags in the sodden and rat-infested trenches, he described to his wife the ground-shaking thump of the artillery, the rat-tat-tat of the machine guns and the sudden illumination of the Very flares overhead. In the middle of this infernal commotion, he blurted out, "Dearest, I yearn for you so, and for the babies and for peace and to cut the grass; and all the little homely things of home."

He kept these desperate longings for safety and home under control. There was no choice: Close friends, nearby, were facing the same strain. His brother-in-law, Jim Macdonnell, already married to Maude's sister Marjorie, was serving in the same salient as an artillery officer, and William went up to watch his battery fire forty-nine eighteen-pound shells in three minutes in an earth-shattering display. Afterward, when the guns were still, he reported to Maude, "we had much good talk, political, philosophical, military." He was determined to sound calm and sanguine.

In the days that followed, he struggled to accustom himself to the nightmarish normality of life around him, reporting to Maude that he would wake, thinking he was still back in England at the training camp, and pick up his toothbrush from the nightstand and go out to wash his teeth, only to step over a covered body, shot through the head, on a stretcher, which would make him realize he was not in England at all.

After just four days to get his bearings, he and his platoon were ordered forward to repair a parapet of trenches that had been knocked down by shellfire, giving the Germans an angle of fire into Canadian lines. Coolly, he drew Maude a picture of the parapet so that she could see what they were being asked to do. He crawled out through a hole in the parapet with another officer and, keeping their heads down, they crawled into a listening post near the German lines. "We could hear Fritz working away behind his parapet about 60 yards off." He could not shake the feeling of the unreality of it all, as if the front were just the firing range at the base back home, but the machine-gun fire sweeping over his head was real enough. The sortie was a success: the parapet was repaired and his superiors congratulated him for a successful mission. He wrote Maude to say that he was hopeful of a battlefield promotion. He had been at the front a week.

The next letter Maude received was not in his hand, but in the hand of a battlefield chaplain in a British dressing station behind the lines.

My dear Maude

I ought to write with my own hand but I am feeling so weak lying here day after day that our good Chaplain who has already written to you for me is going to be my amanuensis.

This is an Imperial Hospital. The one next to it is the Canadian.... We have had all sorts of celebrated visitors. The King and the little Prince were the first. The King smiled upon me graciously and I hope had a fellow feeling for one wounded by a fall from his horse; but seeing I was so weak that day he had the discretion not to speak.

I am not quite sure how my own accident occurred. I was galloping with a loose rein and I think the horse stepped into a shell hole, but as the ground over which I was riding is frequently traversed by spent bullets, one of these may have come in.

When Maude received this letter, she might have thought William would recover quickly. It was only a riding accident, after all. As letter followed letter, first in the handwriting of the chaplain, then in the disjointed scribbles of William himself, she realized that he had suffered serious injuries. His head and chest were in bandages. The horse had been shot out from under him, and had rolled over him, crushing his upper body. He had broken his ribs and there was fluid in his lungs, and for some time both his heart and his liver gave the doctors concern. In the letters the chaplain continued to write on his behalf, William confessed that he was in pain, alone at night in a field hospital with the groans and cries of the wounded around him. He was to remain in the field hospital for two weeks until he was strong enough to be moved to a rear field hospital on the French coast. There George Parkin, using his connections, managed to visit him and reassure his daughter that her husband, though thin as a wraith, was going to pull through.

He was repatriated to Goring to recuperate. Through the autumn of 1916, he was at home with his wife and the little girls, Margaret, Charity and baby Alison. He was soon well enough to derive pleasure from the sight of Alison crawling rapidly and then, with the comic concentration of the very small, pulling herself up and standing at his knee. The doctors told him his lungs would not come right inside of three months, but by Christmas he was well enough to go up to London alone and to stay the night. He went up to see his publisher William Heinemann, who tempted him with heady visions of the profits to be made from a history of the empire. Grant turned him down. Indeed, he was never to write another book. Chapters, speeches, articles continued to come from his pen, but the war brought his scholarly writing career to a close.

On his unsteady first visit to London he went to Harrods, a superior department store, walking around dazed in the bright lights until a female floorwalker took pity on him—"Poor country cousin! Wounded hero if you prefer"—and piloted him to what he was looking for, the racks of military trench coats. By then, the first Zeppelin raids were terrifying London and the city was in blackout. He left the store and stumbled along the Brompton Road in darkness, bumping into strangers, feeling, as he said, "weird and eerie." In the darkened streets, he felt bloodlust rise within him. If he had to endure a month in the blackout, he told Maude, he would "revert to the ape man or the cave-dweller and suddenly club some inoffensive person over the head for sheer lust of lawlessness and desire of blood." The tone is jaunty, but the feeling is taut and strained. It was to take him much longer to recover than he imagined.

He might well have asked to be sent home to Canada. He was forty-four years old. He had been wounded. He had done his duty. But the whole idea was out of the question. At home in Toronto, Vincent Massey, his brother-in-law, was criticized behind his back for rising to the rank of lieutenant colonel without serving in France. William insisted on returning to his unit and, by January 1917, was at a training camp in Hampshire, preparing more boys for their ordeal at the front. Indeed, in the spring of 1917, he was back in France, delivering a unit for service to the front lines, though he never saw combat again.

His own unit, the 20th (Central Ontario) battalion, had moved from the St. Eloi salient up to the base of Vimy Ridge, and between the 9th and 12th of April 1917, it was among the units that made the awe-inspiring ascent of the ridge under fire, capturing a dominating position that had defied the best efforts of other Allied units. Grant would have known many of the men who fought at Vimy—one of his closest friends died there—and he followed the course of events from the Hampshire camp, reporting to his wife on the evening of the 10th of April, "isn't the news from France terrible and splendid?" His battalion was in the thick of the action and its men won eighteen battle honours and two Victoria Crosses in the course of the war. No Canadian unit had a prouder record of service. Eight hundred and fifty-five of the men that Grant trained with, and briefly fought with, never came home.

Ypres, Vimy, Passchendaele. In the horror of these places, Canada's soldiers earned their country its final independence from the British Empire. At the Imperial War Conference of 1917, Canada was recognized as one of the "autonomous nations of the Imperial Commonwealth," and its independent voice in war councils, as a major contributor of men and munitions, was affirmed.

Canadians like Grant entered World War I as loyal colonials. Having fought for the mother country, they slowly realized they were actually fighting for Canada, for its right to be considered a sovereign nation. In the cauldron of war, a new identity was born and an old identity died away. Imperial federation, the ideal for which William's father and his father-in-law gave all their energy, did not survive World War I. In the Imperial conferences of 1926 and in the Statute of Westminster of 1931, Canada secured the right to conduct a fully independent foreign policy and the right to decide for itself whether it would ever be at war again.

By the summer of 1917, William, still in the training camp in Hampshire, received an intriguing offer. Through the intermediary of Vincent Massey, he was offered the principalship of Upper Canada College. At first he told Massey that he couldn't take up the offer until the war was over. In late October, General R.E.W. Turner released him from duty. He had done his part. In November he sailed for Canada, and, in December 1917, having driven a hard bargain with the board of governors—requiring sales of college land in order to boost masters' salaries, plus a substantial salary for himself and housing—he accepted. Maude and the children arrived after him.

Upper Canada College still had its reputation, but by 1917 it was in debt and in decline. Before the war, Grant might have wondered whether he was up to the challenge. But the war had given him confidence. The school turned out to be the place in which he found his true vocation. In his first speech on his installation in December 1917, he made it clear that he was going to transform UCC, beginning with a determined attack on its habit of imitating British ways: "We are and must be a Canadian school and if to be so, we must in any way or in many ways depart from the Etonian tradition, then the break must be made."

The school must borrow from the French methods of language teaching he had admired in Paris. There must be less Latin and Greek, more science and mathematics, less empty exam writing, more sports, more current and world affairs, more scholarships for poor boys. His mind was teaming with ideas. The school must break with the idea that the only thing that mattered was the number of university candidates it graduated. "The boy in whom I take the deepest interest," he said, "is the boy who leaves the school to enter business or industry." He left the school in no doubt that he meant to lead. "I intend to be master in my own house; I intend to rule this school." His goal, he concluded, was to create a school that would mould the men who ruled the nation. And what kind of nation did he dream of?

"A nation of prophets, sages and warriors."

This vision, however overblown it may seem now, would not have seemed so to the boys and masters who listened in the school auditorium that December day. The colonial Canadians who had swept to the top of Vimy

Ridge had proved to the whole world that Canada was indeed a nation of warriors.

Everyone in that hall at his installation address in 1917 would also have known someone who had not returned from France. Some were seared in his own memory. "To ease my own heart," Grant said, he repeated the names of each of his pupils who had perished in France. Of just over a thousand boys from the school who had served overseas, one hundred and fifty-eight had not come back. They must have their memorial, he said, and he proposed that the child of every family who had lost a son in battle must have a free education at the school.

The memory of the war influenced everything he did. If he made sports compulsory for all boys, it was because he believed it was "the sporting spirit which pulled the Empire through the war." If he purchased new rifles and a machine gun for the school Rifle Company, it was because he believed that every boy should have the spit and polish of military drill instilled in him. At his very first address he told the boys the story of a young Canadian officer he knew who, at the Second Battle of Ypres, strode up and down the battle line urging his men out of the trenches with the cry "Come on for Canada! Come on for Canada!"

He was haunted—there is no other word to use—by the memory of the war and by the question of whether those like himself, lucky enough to have survived, were worthy of what they had done. War, he told his students, was the "greatest thing in our experience, sometimes at the back of our minds, sometimes at the front, but always there, consciously or unconsciously shaping our thoughts and actions." Every year he led the school in a memorial service for the fallen, complete with hymns, the trooping of the colours and the reading of the names of the fallen. His speeches to these gatherings were among the most deeply felt he ever delivered.

And so today, I ask you: What welcome shall we give our dead? When the rain patters on the roof, and we hear their crying amid the rain; when the hush falls in crowded church or chapel and their voices are soft in the silence; can we tell them that we have kept faith?

His entire career at Upper Canada can be seen as an attempt to keep the faith with the fallen. It was their example that made him such an impatient public foe of the narrowness of the Ontario high school examination system, such a determined supporter of Frontier College and Workers' Education initiatives for working men in northern Ontario mines and lumber camps; it was why he invited men of the stature of Wilfred Grenfell of the Grenfell Mission in Labrador to lecture the boys on the important public duties that awaited them on graduation. It was why his *History of Canada* for Ontario schools—which went through ten editions in the 1920s and '30s—concluded with a paean to the men who took Vimy Ridge and proved Canada's valour to the world. It was why, no matter what he achieved, there was always more to do. He boosted enrolment, eliminated the debt, enlarged buildings and still remained unsatisfied, remarking in his Prize Day address in 1924, "there is no better education being given in Canada today than that given at UCC—and it is atrocious!"

He chivvied his masters, drove on his pupils and charmed the board of governors to do better, and he knew moments of discouragement, even depression, when he was tempted to quit. But there is no disguising the fact that he had found, in late middle age, his true vocation. Schoolboys the world over have a genius for nicknames, and they gave their principal one that was to stick to him for the rest of his life. They called him Choppy. No one could remember why, but Choppy himself was happy with it.

He hired some extraordinary and eccentric masters: Jock de Marbois, Mauritius born Royal Navy captain and school ski instructor, married to a Russian countess; two music teachers, Ernest MacMillan, later Sir Ernest, and Ettore Mazzoleni, later principal of the Royal Conservatory of Music; and, last but not least, Nicholas Ignatieff, eldest son of a White Russian count, who taught history and politics, chaired the League of Nations club and every summer took boys out west to ride in the Alberta hills. The strategy of eccentricity—of opening an elite school to the new immigration that was changing Canada—was deliberate. As Grant said,

> I am not greatly concerned whether the boys of this school turn out High Tories or Red Tie Socialists; though on the whole I hope they will steer a middle course. I am greatly concerned that they shall not turn out conventional individualists, careful only of their own.

He himself astonished the boys by writing an article for the college magazine on "damn, the finest of expletives." He was seen besting a fellow master at a swearing match. Robertson Davies, one of his pupils, remembered being taken on a walk around the running track with the memorable phrase, "Walk with me and I'll tell you all about the Oscar Wilde scandal." This he proceeded to do with a richness of detail and use of words that Robertson Davies thought only boys knew. He often led the boys in prayer on Sunday nights, and once, he burst out with a paraphrase of Martin Luther that Robertson Davies remembered all his life: "Live in the large! Dare greatly, and if you must sin—sin nobly!"

By now, Maude and William were living in a large house on the college grounds and the long-awaited son, George Parkin Grant, born right after the Armistice of 1918, was named for both his grandfathers. Soon that son was experiencing the special embarrassment of attending his father's school. George Parkin, now Sir George, died in 1922. Maude mourned her father and William completed a biography, begun by Sir John Willison but left unfinished at his death. The chapter on Parkin as headmaster of Upper Canada weaves a delicate path, respectful of his father-in-law's greatness but delicately hinting that a lifetime of oratory in the pulpits of empire had turned his head.

As for the Grant girls, they were attending local schools and playing on the hockey rinks in front of the headmaster's house on the school grounds. In the summers, William and Maude would take the children up to the cottage at Otter Lake, near Georgian Bay, and it was there that he would take them out at night to name the stars.

Deep inside him and then in public utterance, too, his view of the war changed. He now questioned the illusions that had filled his head in 1914. As he told the Upper Canada boys in one of his addresses, "What a world we were going to make! Once the legions of Germany and of her allies had been smashed, how we would go on to smash all the accumulated sins and futilities of the ages. How far away it all seems."

As the Roaring Twenties took hold of Toronto, he now wondered whether the war had achieved anything more than great desolation, followed by heedless consumption and selfishness. He looked about him and saw "an age of easy money"—too many boys had too much of it—and he found it a struggle to hold on to the ideals that had led men to heroic sacrifice. As early as 1919, he concluded a memorial service for the fallen with the words, "One last word, said from my heart. We honour these fallen men.... But let that not lead us to glory war."

He became an outspoken champion of the returning war veterans, spending hours writing letters demanding compensation and medical help for those who came home wounded. He became a supporter of the League of Nations and this, rather than imperial federation, became the ruling cause of his later life. At the memorial address in 1924, he admonished his audience: "We must learn to think internationally and to quench the narrow predatory nationalism which masquerades as patriotism."

He was revisiting and revising the furnace-hot emotions he had felt in August 1914. His son, George, now a teenager, remembered his father's anguished revisions of earlier certainties, this struggle to honour the dead but also to reject war as an instrument of politics.

William carried the war with him in a more direct physical sense. The scarring of his lungs in August 1916 left him vulnerable to colds and infections. In the winter of 1930 and 1931 he came down with pneumonia, and in those days before penicillin and antibiotics, the only remedy the doctor could suggest was to escape the Toronto winter in the Bahamas.

He guided the school successfully through the Depression years and in his Prize Day address in 1934 asked, with characteristic earnestness, "Where are we going when we come out of the Depression? Do those who speak so mean there is good hope that in a few years we shall be repeating the orgy of unthinking prosperity of 1924 to 1929?"

He had been at the job for eighteen years and the college had been transformed: new buildings, facilities, courses, endowment, even a new pension plan for masters. He had taken it from the colonial Eton he had inherited from Parkin and had transformed it into a modern school for an industrial country. Everywhere he looked about him, he could see the monument to his achievement.

In January 1935, he gave a speech to the pupils and then came down with a cold, which quickly developed into pneumonia. On February 3, 1935, the day after his daughter Alison's nineteenth birthday, he died in Toronto General Hospital. He was sixty-two. When they heard the news, the members of the Legislative Assembly of Ontario stood and observed a minute's silence. He was buried in Cataraqui Cemetery in Kingston and shares the same gravestone as his father and mother.

His son, George Parkin Grant, often said that his father had been ruined by the First World War. The Protestant liberal pieties of the Victorian era had not survived the nightmare of the trenches. But this account—of a gentle man living through the ruins of his beliefs and certainties—does not seem right. He was haunted by the war, but the war was also the making of him. It gave him his sense of Canadian vocation, to create a school and, through the school, a country worthy of the men left behind on the fields of France.

In this work, he played his part in the transformation of the myths that were to sustain the Canadian sense of identity in the twentieth century. For his father's generation, the organizing myth had been the conquest of the West and the creation of a continental nation-state. The father lived to see the achievement of that dream in the 1880s, and the son lived to see the closing of the Canadian frontier. In 1918, just back from France, William took a train trip across the country, visiting with Upper Canada and Queen's families who had lost their sons in France. The trip brought home to him that the West of his father's time—the meandering cart tracks through the bush between Hudson's Bay posts, the shale-covered zigzag trails up into the mountains, the Canada of Metis and Cree guides and trappers—had been replaced by a Canada of cities and railway hotels. On his journey, he read an old copy of *Ocean to Ocean* and he decided that he would bring out a new edition when he had a chance. He had his father's book with him when the train stopped, one morning, at Craigellachie. He wrote to Maude that day,

"We both come of good blood, my dear; and it is something to be proud of."

In the place of that common project—the settling and taming of the West—Canada had found, in the First World War, the shared enterprise of defending freedom in Europe and winning, through valour, the respect of the world. The son had played his part in the elaboration of that new myth, the myth that was to be consecrated a year after his death in the gigantic memorial at Vimy.

It is strange, at first sight, that the monument that epitomized Canada's new image of itself in those years should be situated on a hillside in far-off France. But William Grant's life helps to explain why it is not so strange after all. He had left the best of his friends there and struggled to find a meaning in their deaths, not just for himself, but for his country. He found it in an idea of Canada, a vision of the nation as a community of sacrifice. We do not live just for ourselves, but for others, he told his pupils, and there are times when a person has no choice but to fight for the sake for others.

Many Canadians, and not just in Quebec, never shared this vision of their country as a community of sacrifice. Many Canadians still do not. The Vimy ideal does not sit easily with that competing image of Canada as a community of peacemakers, as a country that can show the world how to make a unity of our manifold differences. William Grant's own complex relation to this wartime experience—commemorating the heroic dead, yet pleading with his pupils never to glorify war—testify to his own difficulty in controlling all the implications of Canada as a community of sacrifice. He died unsure not only that these implications could be mastered but also that the memory of Vimy would remain in the hearts of his descendants.

I am his grandson and I attended the ninetieth anniversary of the battle of Vimy in April 2007. The great monument had been cleaned up, the names carved into its plinth had been restored; the two soaring columns and the sculptures of the sorrowing women who guard the site and seem to focus memory in grief held the dying light of day as military buglers sounded a last post. As I looked down into the valley, in the dwindling light, it seemed impossible that men had actually scaled the ridge and had lived to tell the tale.

The next morning dawned bright, and by midday the whole hillside was filled with Canadians—carrying flags, maps of the battle, bags packed with sandwiches and water, guidebooks, cameras and, most importantly, memories and fragments of history they had been told by parents, grandparents, old friends in the Legion Hall and their schoolteachers. As I walked among the crowd, we were not strangers to each other. Everybody wanted to talk about why they were there and what it meant to them. An old woman remembered a brother. An old man remembered a father. Occasionally someone would reach into a backpack and carefully pull out a picture: there he was, in his puttees and service cap, eager, young and now no more. Families had come from all over Canada. They told me that their tours had started with the Normandy beaches, with Juno, and then, if they were from Newfoundland, they had visited the graveyards at Beaumont-Hamel, where the 1st Battalion of the Newfoundland Regiment was cut down. At the base of the hill, men and women walked slowly through the gravestones, bending down, photographing, stopping, placing a flag, writing something down, pausing, then walking on. Always the dates stopped them in their tracks, 1895–1917, 1894–1917, 1900–1917—so horribly young. Beneath some stones without a name engraved upon them lay a shattered body whose identity was known only to God.

Later that afternoon, there were speeches by the prime minister of France, the prime minister of Canada, the Queen and Prince Philip. But I do not remember what they said. It is the crowd I remember, this Canadian crowd, swarming over the hill, searching, looking and affirming something about themselves.

In that crowd were several thousand high school students, mostly from Ontario towns, but some also from out West and down East. Some wore T-shirts imprinted with the picture of a soldier from the Great War. Others carried social studies notebooks with the research they had done on a single soldier who had died at Vimy. Their teachers had assigned Vimy as their winter history assignment, and they fanned out over the hill, disappearing into the network of tunnels and trenches that are still kept open to remind people what the Canadians faced as they came up the hill under fire.

The speeches and the ceremony were held in a field below the monument, and just before the events began, the students and their teachers came down the road that winds around the monument down to the field below. As they did so, we could hear them singing "O Canada!," thousands of young voices all together, the sound echoing against the monument, filling the air and stilling every other voice. It was a moment of affirmation—these young Canadians marching around the monument, singing their country's anthem—that would have made William Grant's heart glad.

4
LAMENT FOR A
NATION

George Grant was sixteen when his father died. Within a year, the family had scattered: Alison to London, where she was to remain until 1945; Margaret to marriage and a young family with Geoffrey Andrew, a teacher at Upper Canada College; Charity to social work in Toronto; and their mother to a job as superintendent of the Royal Victoria College, a women's college at McGill University in Montreal. As for George, he followed in his father's footsteps to Queen's University in Kingston.

At Upper Canada College, he had been the principal's son. At Queen's he was the grandson of Principal Grant. In his mother's eyes, he was the longed-for bearer of the family lineage. Both lineages—the Grants and the Parkins—were forbidding inheritances for a bereaved teenager. From both sides of the family, he was told he must excel, he must prove himself worthy.

He always said that it was his mother who tightened the vise of family expectation, who imbued him with a sense that he had to measure up to the ancestors. He adored her and resented the pressure of her expectations in equal measure. All his life he remained astonishingly needy for Maude's love, which he felt, despite all evidence to the contrary, she withheld. With surprising candour, he confessed in later life to an enduring, even monstrous, Oedipus complex.

George's memories of his father were a complex blend of condescension and respect. He was condescending about his father's temperament, seemingly so gentle and genial, while George himself was all passionate conviction, consequences be damned. At the same time, he respected his father's judgment of people, his quietly scathing view of his brother-in-law, Vincent Massey, as an ambitious social climber, his view of Liberal prime minister Mackenzie King as a sentimental but ruthless mediocrity. George knew his father was a liberal, both small L and big L, who sometimes voted for the socialist CCF from sheer exasperation with King. But King was not the only embodiment of liberalism. George remembered listening with his father to Franklin D. Roosevelt's inaugural speech in 1933 on the radio in Grant House, with that immortal phrase "there is nothing to fear but fear itself." The speech deeply moved his father with its vindication not only of faith in the republic, but of faith in politics itself. Whatever hostility George later displayed toward

American liberalism, whatever scorn he heaped on the Canadian variant, it was tempered by the memory of what Roosevelt had meant to his father.

George must also have heard his father's Upper Canada chapel sermons, particularly those that dwelt on the futility of war and the need to turn away from war as an instrument of politics. George used to say that his father had been ruined by the war, although it would have been truer to say that it was in the war that Choppy found his way. The same would prove true of the son. Like his father, he found himself in London in wartime and, as for his father, this time proved decisive in the making of his view of Canada and of his role as a Canadian.

In 1939 George won the Rhodes Scholarship and chose his father's old Oxford college, Balliol. One can imagine what this would have meant to a grandson of Sir George Parkin, the founding secretary of the scholarships and a Balliol man himself. His mother, Maude, took the twenty-year-old to New York, treated him to a perform-ance of Lillian Hellman's *The Little Foxes* and waved goodbye to him on the USS *Manhattan,* bound for Liverpool.

He reached Oxford a month after war was declared. Already at Queen's George's pacifist convictions, built on his father's own disillusionment with the Great War, had taken root. Within weeks of arriving at Oxford, they had become the guiding principle of his actions. He fell in with a group of Christian and socialist pacifists who believed that no matter who won, the war would destroy Western civilization. Their consciences forbade them to take a life or share patriotic attachment to any country conceived as a community of sacrifice.

Shortly after his twenty-first birthday, George decided he would have no part in a war he regarded as an orgy of destructive mania let loose upon the world. Yet he knew that he could not return home to safety in Canada. He would either enlist in an ambulance brigade or serve as a fire warden.

His decision was a crucial break with a family tradition that had always welcomed service to king and country as the ultimate test of its Canadian patriotism. And it was a decision that sharply divided the family. Back home, his uncle Jim Macdonnell—who had fought at the Somme with George's father—was furious. Mrs. Buck, a wealthy admirer of Sir George Parkin, who had once intimated that she would leave her fortune to George, now threatened to bar him from her mansion on the Welsh borders.

George's uncle Vincent Massey was in London as Canada's high commissioner. His wife, Alice—known as Aunt Lal—was his mother's favourite sister. Their own sons, Hart and Lionel, had enlisted for service. The Masseys struggled to understand their nephew's refusal to do so. George's sister Alison tried to be sympathetic, but she had already made a different choice by enrolling at an ambulance station and soon taking work at the British War Office. The man Alison was to marry—George Ignatieff—had abandoned his Rhodes Scholarship, sought to enlist in the British Army and was now working at Canada House as Vincent Massey's assistant. His brother, Nicholas Ignatieff, was due to arrive shortly to work in the Russian section of British military intelligence. The brightest Canadian diplomats of their generation, Charles Ritchie and Lester "Mike" Pearson, both well known to George's mother, were also serving in Canada House. Everyone whom George knew was on active duty or in military service.

Between the Dunkirk evacuation of May and June 1940 and the arrival of American soldiers and airmen in the spring of 1942, Canadians played a uniquely important role in the defence of Britain. The Canadian division commanded by General Andrew McNaughton was one of the largest military units left intact after the defeat and evacuation of the British Army from France. To aid the British war effort, munitions poured out of Canadian factories. Food from Canadian farms arrived by the shipload on the North Atlantic convoys. Canada had never been so important to the survival of the British Isles. Just as in World War I, Canada entered the war two years before the Americans. George himself commented on the significance of this in an essay in 1945:

We are a country of 1914 and 1939 rather than 1917 and 1941. Both times we were the first country of the American continent to take responsibility for the rest of the world. Both times the fact that we were taking such responsibility influenced the U.S.A.

For the young Canadians who lived through the Battle of Britain in London, the sense that Canada stood alone with Britain in its hour of need defined their view of Canada ever after. They came away with a vivid sense that Canada mattered in the world, but they also became starkly aware of the mother country's vulnerability. They knew that Britain could not win without the Americans, and they fervently believed that Roosevelt would find a way to get America into the war soon. In the meantime, while they waited, they were bemused by some American reactions to the conflict. During the bombing of London, Alison Grant happened upon an old copy of *The New York Times* and found American sentimentality about the brave British under fire rather grating. There was, she wrote to a friend in Toronto, "a rather smug sense of admiration for us which exasperated me. There is nothing like the heroism we are showing to bring tears to the eyes of a lot of Americans." In this context—Canada alone standing beside Britain, Canadian soldiers thronging the streets of London in uniform, every member of his family actively working for Allied victory—George's decision to reject military service and to serve as an air raid warden took an almost perverse determination, certainly in someone barely twenty-one years of age. In the face of whispered disapproval, false pity and outright condemnation, George remained undeterred.

In September 1940, he moved to Bermondsey in south London. He knew the Oxford and Bermondsey Club in Tanner Street, near London Bridge Station, where, before the war, Oxford undergraduates had come down on vacations to work with the poor in the surrounding streets. The club provided a soup kitchen and a social club, as well as a medical mission. George lived in Bermondsey between September 1940 and August 1941, taking his meals at the soup kitchen, sleeping in the air raid shelters under the railway arches, serving as a shelter warden and then as a member of the local ARP, the air raid precautions service. During that time, Bermondsey was under almost continuous nightly bombardment from German aircraft targeting the London docks. Some of his letters to his mother were written while a "real rocker of a raid" was underway. George taught evening classes in the shelters and organized a boxing club for teenage boys. When the raids were over, he went out into the blazing streets and extinguished the fires from incendiary bombs with water and sand. He rescued families from bombed-out houses; he identified dead bodies and took them to the morgue. In a letter written in 1941, he looked back blankly:

> I helped wounded people—I carried the dead—I evacuated shelters—I lost some good friends—I told people that their relatives were in hospital when I had just seen them taken to the morgue. I told others the truth. For myself I was up 36 hours on end and while it lasted was very near death. I put out innumerable incendiaries.

He lived the most intense months of his life in Bermondsey. At first, his dominant feeling was sheer exhilaration. For the first time in his life, he was nobody's son or grandson. To his surprise, people accepted him for who he was. A woman in a shelter knitted him a sweater. Another woman, the wife of an airman, leaned against him in the shelter one night and whispered "Stay," and he did. Working men bought him drinks in The Raven and The Sun pub or slipped him a pack of cigarettes. The cook at the Oxford and Bermondsey Club, Mrs. Lovett, a wild and amusing Irishwoman with an errant husband and seven children, was soon feeding George and looking after him. The people of Bermondsey took to George because, unlike most of the Oxford undergraduates who showed up at the Oxford and Bermondsey Club, he actually remained at their side through the bombardment. George was, for a time, in love with them all, with what they represented, the incarnation of England at its best. The sublime calm of some of the people he helped out of the rubble stayed with him forever. As he wrote his mother,

> Granny Peck was just bombed out a second time. It was too much. She sat by the fire, but I knew she was dying; so I sent for the doctor. He got an ambulance and Granny put on her wonderful black bonnet & her cane & her bag of treasures—her whole life of wonderful things of all kinds. She walked down with me. We lifted her into the ambulance. I kissed her and said "Goodbye Gran." All she said was "Don't say goodbye; it's just au revoir." She looked so calm & lovely—and a week later she died.

In one letter home to his mother, he exclaimed, "God I have learned more about loving from these people than any others." How his mother reacted to that wounding remark one can only imagine.

He lived a double life, as escape from Bermondsey was only a bus ride away. His aunt Lal remembered him showing up at her office in the Dorchester Hotel, "black in the face with smut and dirt of all the hours' work he had gone through, wet boots, wet clothes." He would shower and then return to Bermondsey. When once again he was too grimy, exhausted or shell-shocked to continue, he would take the bus across London to 231 Sussex Gardens, near Paddington Station, for a bath, a meal and bed at the flat his sister Alison shared with the Greey sisters, Mary and Elizabeth. Occasionally, Mary or Alison would visit him in Bermondsey and bring news of him to Uncle Vincent and Aunt Lal. Mike Pearson too went down to Bermondsey and reported to the Masseys that their nephew was doing a "marvellous job." The word was passed back in Canada that no one should question George's courage.

Uncle Jim, however, continued to do just that and Mrs. Buck maintained that his only salvation lay in immediate enlistment in the British Army. George countered by asking her to billet some Bermondsey evacuees on her estate. She refused, furthering his conviction that the patriotism around him was hypocritical and false.

In February 1941, he proudly showed Burgon Bickersteth, one of his mother's oldest friends and warden of Hart House at the University of Toronto, around Stayners, the shelter where he worked under the arches of London Bridge Station. Hurricane lamps hung from the rafters, the shelter was crowded with sleeping families, and he and George spent the night there on the bunk beds, being wakened the next morning by Mrs. Lovett with a cup of tea.

On Monday, February 17, 1941, while George was away, Stayners Shelter sustained a direct hit. Hundreds of people were killed. George's letter home five days later is still numb with the shock:

My railway arch was hit and most of my friends in Bermondsey were eliminated or in hospital; so there it is. I was out, but came back to find it after it had happened. I thought I had seen the worst, but this was the end.

Mrs. Lovett survived and helped him through the shock, but everyone noticed, in Aunt Lal's words, that "he now began to pay the price." He fell into a deepening crisis of what we would now recognize as post-traumatic shock and depression. His letters home took on a bitter, even spiteful tone, sarcastically exclaiming how glad he was that Mike Pearson had told his family that he had been doing well. He complained that no one in the West End seemed to care about the East End, not even his sister Alison. He seemed to forget that she, too, had been bombed, had put out incendiaries, rescued belongings from the ruins of the bombed-out houses of friends. He believed that only he had borne the true brunt of the war and he could not get over what he had lived through. He wandered through the streets of Bermondsey, thinking here he had picked up the remains of Mr. Grey the newsagent, there was the place where the Peeneys' house once stood, here he had caught a looter, there he had doused an incendiary. He meditated darkly in his letters about "the tiger-like violence" of the high explosive and wondered why he had been spared.

By June 1941, he was frequenting "revolutionary" cells in Bermondsey and grimly informing his mother that when the war was over, the old gentle liberal England she had known would be finished, too. Yet he did not throw in his lot with these left-wing groups. "I can see no brave new world coming from them," he reported home. If anything, he began to repent of his earlier infatuation with the people of Bermondsey: "The working classes of this country are just as corrupt as the people above them." Even the people of Bermondsey, he said, were filled with imperialist superiority toward so-called lesser peoples. If there was to be a future for Europe after the war, he wrote home, Europe would have to realize it was not "heaven-endowed to run the world." The British war effort, he exclaimed, was built on a lie: "the giant defender of freedom maintaining the greatest and most barbaric of empires."

With Hitler's invasion of Russia in June 1941, the bombing of London ceased and George felt renewed pressure to enlist, now that his work as an ARP warden had come to an end. The pressure seems mostly to have come from inside himself. His cousin Lionel Massey had been captured in Greece and was now a prisoner of war in Germany. Hitler was marching toward Moscow. Though George continued to refer to the war as a "cauldron of folly and stupidity, pride and selfishness"—from which fastidious free thinkers should stand apart—it must have begun to seem self-deluding to think so.

At the end of August 1941, he wrote his mother that he had decided to enlist in the merchant marine, calling it "one of the stupidest, most useless, basest actions of his life," but one forced upon him by the sheer pressure of family expectation. By enlisting, he had in effect repudiated his pacifism. He added bitterly that he was a slave of his baptism.

In reality, he was the slave of no one. His family had been more than understanding of the position he had taken. It was his own demons that were propelling him now. He moved out of Bermondsey and into the Dorchester Hotel with the Masseys. In October 1941, he set off for Middlesbrough in the north of England to join a merchant ship. Before boarding he learned, in a routine medical exam, that he had a tubercular lesion on his lung and was unfit for service. In a panic, he vanished from sight, headed for Liverpool, tried to sign on to another ship, was rebuffed and instead worked in demolition on the docks. In late November he returned to the Oxford area and found a job working as a farm labourer near Aylesbury. All this time, his family went without news of him. On December 7, 1941, he woke to the news that the Japanese had attacked Pearl Harbor. For most people, especially his family, the fact that America would enter the war meant that victory was assured, however long it might take. For a pacifist like George, the news that the war he had opposed would now become a global struggle came as a disorienting blow. For four days, he later remembered, he felt close to suicide. Then, on December 11 or 12, riding his bicycle along the narrow country roads outside of Aylesbury as the dawn rose, he stopped to unlock one of the gates placed across the road to stop cattle, and as he walked his bicycle through and closed the gate behind him, he knew, at once and for a certainty, that God existed and that all was well. This private epiphany—lasting an instant—proved to be the decisive event of his life.

The family had not heard from him for almost four months when he suddenly turned up one night in January 1942 at 54A Walton Street in Knightsbridge, the flat above a dairy where his sister Alison was living with another Canadian, Kay Moore. He was gaunt, dirty, badly dressed and both volatile and depressed. For the next month, he exhausted Kay's and Alison's patience with his lack of cleanliness, his overwhelming neediness and his aggressive bouts of self-justification. It was obvious he had to go home. In February he returned by Atlantic convoy to Canada. His mother took him in at the house she had inherited from Lady Parkin, at 7 Prince Arthur Avenue in Toronto. For the rest of 1942 and the first months of 1943, he remained at home with his mother, reading, grieving for the people he had lost in the raids on Bermondsey and trying to get his life back in order.

In 1943, he got a job with the Canadian Association of Adult Education and began a lifelong association with the CBC, preparing the Citizens' Forum broadcasts hosted by Morley Callaghan. By early 1945 he was writing "Have

We a Canadian Nation?" which outlined, for the first time, the theory that Canada was a conservative nation, based on adherence to "sane and orthodox religions rooted in the past" together with British institutions. He saw Canada as a middle way between the liberal acquisitive individualism of the United States and the collective tyranny of the Soviet experiment. In early 1945, he published a pamphlet, *The Empire, Yes or No,* in which he maintained that Canada could survive as an independent state only within the British Commonwealth. Otherwise Canada could not maintain its identity beside the United States.

The Empire, Yes or No also recanted his pacifism:

> In 1940 we saw that it was not the pious talk of idealists that stopped fascism and the forces of evil, it was the practical co-operation of free nations of the British Commonwealth. Some always knew this lesson; some learned it very late (like this writer). But let us all remember it after the war, and never forget it.

While he recanted his stance on the war, pacifism continued to shape his attitude toward nuclear weapons. He was just returning to England in 1945 when the bomb was dropped on Hiroshima. It remained for him the purest example of technological evil in the service of American imperialism. His opposition to American nuclear weapons on Canadian soil—which inspired *Lament for a Nation*—can be traced back to his pacifism and to his encounter with the destructive power of high explosives in Bermondsey.

By way of contrast, the other Canadians in London drew a very different lesson from their experiences. In the autumn of 1940, Mike Pearson and George Ignatieff were fire-watching on the roof of Canada House as incendiaries landed on the roofs all around Trafalgar Square. As they stared out at London on fire, Ignatieff remembered Mike Pearson saying that this could not go on and that the indiscriminate bombardment of civilian populations would mean the end of civilization itself. There had to be a better way. After the war, he and Ignatieff threw themselves into the creation of the United Nations, and then, as the Cold War developed, the creation of the North Atlantic Treaty Organization. In 1956, they worked together for the deployment of the first UN peacekeepers in Sinai, for which Pearson was awarded the Nobel Peace Prize. In contrast to the Christian conservative pacifism of George Grant, they embraced a liberal anti-communist internationalism. In contrast to George, they believed in an essential difference, at once political and moral, between Stalinist tyranny and American imperial hegemony, while George continued to argue, right into the 1960s, that there was no real difference between Canadian subservience to the United States and the position of Soviet satellites such as Poland, Hungary and Czechoslovakia.

George's sister Alison spent the entire war in London, moving from the War Office into MI5, British Military Intelligence. In late 1942 and early 1943, she came to know a young Canadian, Frank Pickersgill, who had been studying at the Sorbonne in Paris when war was declared. Like George, Frank had stood aside from the war and he had remained in France until the German invasion of 1940. He escaped occupied France in 1942, made his way to London and, after what he had seen of the Gestapo during internment, enrolled immediately in the Special Operations Executive for clandestine operations. While training as a saboteur, parachutist and signals operator, he and his fellow trainee, John Macalister, spent the weekends at 54A Walton Street with Kay Moore and Alison Grant. Alison fell in love with Frank. In June 1943, Frank and John were dropped by night into occupied France. They were captured within a week and imprisoned in France. Alison spent 1943 and 1944 hoping against hope that Pickersgill and Macalister would survive, only to learn in the summer of 1945 that they had been tortured and executed in the concentration camp at Buchenwald in late 1944. It was a shattering blow, but she never doubted that Frank had done the right thing or thought that she or anyone else could have stopped him from doing what he had to do. She taught her children to revere Frank's example. George once wrote of Frank that courage such as Pickersgill's was a virtue before which one can only bow.

In August 1945, George Grant returned to Oxford to resume his Rhodes Scholarship. He met up with Alison, then preparing to return home to Canada. He noticed that she seemed depressed and withdrawn, even angry with him for having left England three years earlier. He wrote his mother, urging her to treat her gently upon her return. He had no idea that she had just learned of Frank's death.

The relationship between brother and sister never recovered from the war. George had made his choices. Alison had made hers, and in Frank's example, she found the polar star of her ultimate allegiances.

When George told his mother that he was returning to Oxford not to study law or politics but to study theology, he remembered her exploding with all the pent-up frustration of a mother who had seen the son in whom she had placed all her hopes crack under the strain of war. "George, you have always been the poseur of the family, but this is the worst pose of all," she raged.

It was not a pose but the beginning of a decisive change in his life. He explained to her that he had to study theology because "my need for God is … overwhelming."

This need for God had changed him. And England had changed, too. He renewed his friendship with Mrs. Lovett and welcomed the Labour victory of July 1945 as a victory for Bermondsey. But he did not share the enthusiasm of his socialist friends for the new government. His ever-deepening religious faith was convincing him of the futility of salvation through politics. This lofty fatalism about the relevance of political action was already deeply embedded in his intellectual makeup by 1945.

He continued to think of England as the civilized, ancient alternative to the brutal new empires of America and Russia, but as 1945 turned into 1946 and 1947 and he ploughed along with his doctoral dissertation, Canada began to pull him home. He told his mother, "I love England—and think it is the greatest country on earth— [but] Canada is in one's heart in a way that this country can never be." Yet finding work at home for a young man with an unfinished doctorate proved difficult. Burgon Bickersteth and the Masseys proposed him for the position of warden of Hart House, the campus student centre at the University of Toronto, then filled with returning veterans. The committee considering the appointment decided they couldn't select someone who had not served. George was philosophical. "You cannot have the plums after being a pacifist." Nicholas Ignatieff, then returning from Britain after service in military intelligence, was chosen instead. George accepted a job teaching philosophy at Dalhousie University in Halifax and, after marrying Sheila Allen, who was to deepen his faith and to strengthen his convictions, he began his career as a Christian conservative philosopher in Canada.

Despite having broken with the family on the issue of service to king and country, he remained faithful to the

Parkin and Grant heritage in other respects. He continued to subscribe to his father's and grandfather's essential belief that Canadian identity could not survive without a British core. But already in his twenties, he was giving the family credo a new inflection: conservative, religious, hostile to progress, modernity and liberalism. This was a substantial act of revision, even falsification, of his own heritage. His grandfather Grant, together with Sandford Fleming, had welcomed the leading technologies of the age—the railway and the undersea cable—as tools for nation building. George himself had been left Sandford Fleming's watch, the first watch, he liked to tell interviewers, that Fleming installed with twenty-four-hour time. George valued the watch but not what it signified. Technology of this transformative sort was no longer progressive. He had seen what high explosives could do to an air raid shelter, and he never again associated technology with progress.

He revised his own pacifism, but he did not revisit his view that the war had laid bare the essentially inhuman dynamic of industrial capitalism. The war experience left him convinced that technology had become the master, not the servant, of the human soul.

He also came to believe, through the spiritual crisis he experienced during the war, that Christian faith was the core of his being and that Western civilization could not be redeemed without a return to faith. This view of modernity was deepened by his reading of the French philosopher and thinker Simone Weil. Though they never met, she too had been in wartime London and, like him, had been tormented by the conflict between a pure Christian pacifism and her awareness, as a Jew fleeing occupied Europe, that she must do something to confront evil. Her war work, her attempt to provide de Gaulle's free French with a blueprint for postwar reconstruction in France, was a book called *The Need for Roots: Prelude to a Declaration of Duties towards Mankind.* It was first published at the end of the war, after her death in 1943 in a tuberculosis sanatorium in Ashford, Kent. The book's message paralleled George's conviction that a war-wounded world could be healed only by returning both to community—local, particular, rooted—and to faith—Christian, transcendent and purifying.

Under the influence of Weil and his wife's strong religious belief, George came to conclude that the family's original faith—pious, earnest Presbyterianism—had been the spine that had sustained both its patriotic love of Canada and its insistence that Canada must resist the lure of American ideals and greed. Once this spine of faith had dissolved, the family tradition degenerated into an empty, secular liberalism that offered no resistance to American influences. Whether this was true or not did not matter. What mattered was that he believed it and drew the conclusion that it was up to him to salvage the family's intellectual inheritance from the shallow liberal conformity into which it had subsided.

Another decisive factor that shaped the evolution of George's thought after the war was the changing place of Canada in the world. The Canadians of his generation forged in the crucible of wartime London—Ritchie, Pearson, the Masseys, his sister, the Ignatieffs—returned to the peacetime world with a deep sense that Canada mattered. Anyone who had lived through wartime London and the Canadian part in victory—from Dieppe through Juno, through the liberation of Holland—knew that we were a serious country, with a serious part to play in the making of the postwar world.

Because George, like them, had lived in London at the height of Canada's brief moment—after Dunkirk but before Pearl Harbor—it came as a shock that the United States had emerged the victor and that Britain was subsiding into war-ravaged decline. This changed everything the Grant family had assumed about the place of Canada in the world. Canada's fate had been tied to the fortunes of the British Empire. What would it do now as the mother country found herself eclipsed by the American ascendancy? As George settled into the prosperous Canada of the 1950s, teaching at Dalhousie and then at McMaster University, he was appalled that the Canada he had grown up in—Protestant small town, British, virtuous—was being swept away by a surge of continental integration. To his dismay, much of central Canada began to look like anywhere in the United States, with the same highways, gas stations and supermarkets. Instead of questioning whether this tide of continental integration was a good thing, Canadians seemed to embrace it. And worst of all, the Liberal Party of Canada, led by C.D. Howe, Louis St. Laurent and Mike Pearson, appeared to welcome rather than resist the Americanizing tide. It was especially bitter to see old friends like Pearson appearing to abet the assimilationist drift.

In 1963, George's mother, Maude Parkin Grant, died at eighty-two after five years lost in the white desert of Alzheimer's disease. By the end, if she acknowledged him at all, she mistook her son for her father, George Parkin. The woman he had called his anchor, the last living connection with the Parkin and Grant tradition, was now gone.

Two days after her death, the Liberal Party, led by Mike Pearson, combined with the other opposition parties to bring down the Conservative government of John Diefenbaker. The issue on which Diefenbaker fell was his refusal to allow American nuclear weapons—the Bomarc missile—on Canadian soil.

In another single, defining moment—the death of his beloved mother, the severing of the last link with the ancestors, the perceived sellout of Canada by an old friend and the introduction of American weapons onto Canadian soil—Grant saw what he must do. Over the next year, he composed *Lament for a Nation,* a ninety-seven-page polemic that was, as he put it, "a celebration of … the memory of that tenuous hope that was the principle of my ancestors." Diefenbaker's fall was the pretext, but the deeper source of the essay's extraordinary rhetorical power was his sense that a great tradition of patriotic identification with Canada, central to his being, had been betrayed by those, like Pearson, whom he had once considered friends.

The thesis of *Lament for a Nation* was simple and stark. Canada had gone from colony to nation to colony, from imperial subservience to Britain to imperial subservience to the United States. In the process, it had lost its identity and its soul. Its disappearance was only a matter of time.

But this was not all. The new empire of capitalism and commerce subverted all the smaller, local and provincial attachments that once went by the name of love of country. In the era of technological modernity, love of country was a sentimental and retrograde illusion. A place like Canada could no longer serve as an object of love and longing.

Lament for a Nation appeared the year I began my undergraduate career at the University of Toronto. I rebelled against this pessimism then, as I do today. But George Grant's pessimism lays down the gauntlet. There is no easy answer to the challenge he posed—for he asked, as no one had ever done before, Is Canada still possible?

He defended Diefenbaker and the Conservatives, he said, because, unlike the Liberals, "the character of Canada as British North America was in their flesh and bones." He added that many men in the Conservative Cabinet had been men of the 1939 war, as if this was proof of their loyalty to Britain, conveniently forgetting that he had been the pacifist and that "the ambitious little bureaucrat"—his acidic description of Pearson—had been a man who had served in both the First and Second World Wars. George was equally scathing about Pearson's men—who now included his brother-in-law, George Ignatieff, who had married Alison in 1945—calling them acquiescent servants of American imperialism. Ignatieff, who had preceded George Grant as a Rhodes Scholar at Balliol and was now working in the Canadian foreign service in Ottawa, did not enjoy George's remark that "the officials of External Affairs had mostly been educated in the twilight scepticism of Oxford liberalism." In George's hands, "liberalism" became a catch-all term of abuse, a synonym for value-free secularism and supine acquiescence to the American takeover.

To the world outside the Grant-Ignatieff families, *Lament* was a masterpiece of rhetorical invective, accusing the entire civil service establishment of Liberal Ottawa of a *trahison des clercs*, a betrayal of Canada to the Americans. Inside the family, *Lament* was seen as a reckless reckoning, with slights imagined and real, going back to wartime London.

Canadian socialists and left-wingers loved the book's denunciation of the civil service, the branch-plant economy and the dependence of the Canadian capitalist class on their American masters. For all the left-wing rhetoric—which had been a feature of George's thinking since his time among the socialists and communists of Bermondsey—*Lament*'s real purpose was to reappropriate the family tradition as a defence of a conservative Christian Canada. He sought to channel the voices of the ancestors, but in doing so, he gave them his own voice alone. Neither his grandfather nor his father had ever been so uniformly negative about the Americans, so hostile to science and technology and everything that went by the name of progress. His grandfather Grant had opposed trade reciprocity with the Americans in the election of 1891, but his father, William, had been in favour of it in the election of 1911. To say that the family spoke with one voice—against economic integration with the United States—was never true. To say that Canada could only be conservative or it could not exist had never been the ancestral doctrine. But in George's act of ventriloquism, the ancestors spoke, and they spoke in support of *his* vision of Canada.

In doing so, however, George emptied the tradition of any capacity to inspire hope and faith in the country's future. If Canada could exist only as a conservative country, and if liberals had sold it out to the Americans, with the complicity of most Canadians, what hope remained? Precious little. He had voided the ancestral traditions of what had been central to them, namely a faith that Canada could shape and master its own destiny. If politics and political action were futile, where were Canadians to look for salvation? George took refuge in his own religious faith, forgetting that this consolation was not necessarily available to most of his readers. The concluding paragraph of *Lament* ended in a note of otherworldly bleakness:

> Those who loved the older traditions of Canada may be allowed to lament what has been lost.... Multitudes of human beings through the course of history have had to live when their only political allegiance was irretrievably lost. What was lost was often something far nobler than what Canadians have lost. Beyond courage, it is also possible to live in the ancient faith, which asserts that changes in the world, even if they be recognized more as a loss than a gain, take place within an eternal order that is not affected by their taking place.

Lament's last line is a quotation from Virgil: *Tendebantque manus ripae ulterioris amore*. "They were holding their arms outstretched in love toward the further shore." If the ancestral traditions were calling us ever more faintly from an ever-increasing distance, then politics in Canada was finished, and all that was left was the consolation of faith.

Only politics wasn't finished. Everywhere anybody looked in 1965, the year *Lament* appeared, a generation of students and radicals was trying to stop the war in Vietnam. I invited my famous uncle to address a teach-in at the University of Toronto in 1965. I vividly remember the impression made by this gigantic figure, who appeared like a bearded patriarch, though he was only forty-six at the time. He stood before a crowd of five thousand people in Varsity Arena and announced, "I speak as a Canadian nationalist and as a conservative." We should rage against the dying of the Canadian light, he told the crowd, but we should be under no illusions that it is dying. Even if the war in Vietnam could be ended, the impulses that had created the war—the American drive for imperial mastery propelled by the liberal faith in technology—were woven so deep into the psyches of even those who opposed the war that purging North American civilization of these imperatives was futile. Holding on to the vestigial, minor differences that distinguished Canada from the United States was hardly worth the political effort. He concluded that speech in 1965 with a dark admonition.

Hope in the future has been and is the chief opiate of modern life. Its danger is that it prevents men from looking clearly at their situation.... Moral fervour is too precious a commodity not to be put into the service of reality.

The Canadians who heard him that day believed he was actually calling for a revival of Canadian nationalism, and they took him at his word. He may have counselled fatalism but, happily, Canadians did not listen. Ironically, he played his part in reviving a political debate about Canada and its relation to the United States that endures to this day.

He made the mistake of believing that the differences that separated the culture of liberty in Canada and the United States were vestigial and doomed to die away. But they were more stubborn and substantial differences than he supposed, and the defence of them has proved successful.

America and Canada are both free nations. But our freedom is different: there is no right to bear arms north of the 49th parallel, and no capital punishment either; we believe in collective rights to language and land, and, in our rights culture, these can trump individual rights. Not so south of the border. Rights that are still being fought for south of the border—public health care, for example— have been ours for a generation. These differences are major, and George Grant's conclusion that they were minor misunderstood Canadian history and our enduringly different political tradition.

His second mistake was to believe that since we had lost the anchorage of Britain, we had lost the feature that distinguished us from the Americans. This had been the ruling illusion of both his grandfather and his father—that Britishness defined of who we were as a people.

But we had never just been British. Our myths of origin are plural, not singular. We have three competing ones, English, French and Aboriginal. Three peoples share a state and a land. George Grant paid almost no attention to the constitutive role of the Aboriginals and Metis in Canadian identity and tended to regard *la survivance* of Quebec as a noble but dying vestige of the pre-industrial era.

The third mistake was that he gave up on his country at exactly the moment when it roused itself to action. At the moment of *Lament*'s appearance, Canada went through the most extraordinary reinvention of its identity in history. And to no one's surprise but his own, much of the impetus behind this was inspired by the party he detested, the Liberal Party of Canada. In the twenty years after *Lament for a Nation* was published, Canada staged Expo 67, the most triumphant affirmation of Canadian pride before or since; we had the Quiet Revolution and the resurgent reaffirmation of Quebec identity in North America; we had the promotion of official bilingualism; the modern Canadian welfare state—medicare and the Canada Pension Plan—was created, distinguishing us ever more sharply from the United States; we had the repatriation of the Canadian constitution, the next-to-last symbol of our dependency on the British, and the creation of the Charter of Rights and Freedoms, incarnating a distinctive national rights culture; and we gave ourselves a national anthem and a flag. And last but not least, we opened our doors to immigration from the four corners of the world, transforming the population and internationalizing our identity as never before.

We are still taking the measures of these changes, but no reasonable person can look at Canada in the fifty years since the publication of *Lament for a Nation* and conclude that the Canadian identity is weaker now than it was in 1965.

Yes, we've gone into free trade with the United States and, as we did so, we feared assimilation, loss of identity and loss of sovereignty. Can we honestly say these fears have been realized?

And as for George's larger argument about the impact of global consumer capitalism on national consciousness in general, the remarkable feature of modernity is not the erosion of local, national attachments, but, on the contrary, the reassertion of ethnicity, language and race as markers of national identity in the modern world.

To paraphrase Isaiah Berlin, the bent twig of national identity, pushed down by the forces of global commerce, the American way of life and communist tyranny, snapped back with the end of the Cold War, and everywhere you looked—whether it was the former Yugoslavia, Quebec, the Basque country, Scotland or the Middle East—a passionate resurgence of ethnic, religious, tribal and local identities had rewritten the history Grant had thought was leading us to imperial domination and cultural uniformity.

So he was wrong. Wrong. Wrong again.

And yet *Lament for a Nation* remains a masterpiece of grief and anger. It continues to speak to an elemental anxiety about our country, that sense that there is not enough here to make a great country. For the imperialists in the family, greatness would come to Canada if it aligned its destiny with an imperial British future. Their grandson George saw this future die in wartime London, as a battered England surrendered its hegemony to the arriving Americans. He then asked, If the dream was done, what would replace it as the guiding mythology of his native land? Around him he felt the American way of life sweeping away the small-town Canada he so loved. Against this gathering wave, he could mount only a cry of despair.

The family tradition from which he spoke, and which lives in me and my generation, need not end in lament. He gave up on the country. He should not have. The country is not done. The story has only just begun. There is so much more to tell, so much more to do.

I last saw my uncle George and my aunt Sheila in the small, cramped front room of their house on Walnut Street in Halifax in June 1983. I was a young academic then and I had come to town for the Learned Society meetings. Every few minutes as I sat with them, another student from the past would knock on the door and be admitted to sit with him. Some of them were very young, and some were very distinguished, but they all sat in reverent awe as he held forth, this great shambling patriarch with a straggly beard and a huge laugh that revealed a frightful set of crooked and stained teeth. His visitors came to be in his presence, and he was gracious and regal with all. By then, he was loaded with honours, including degrees and the gold medal of the Royal Society of Canada. The old lion had finally been accepted by Canadian academic life as one of its great ones.

When we were left alone, I talked, with gingerly care, about some work I had been doing on Jean-Jacques Rousseau, worried that I might bait the bear with liberal provocations. He didn't take the bait, and we shared our love of Rousseau's demonic, extreme, visionary side. I didn't venture onto conflicted ground, his and Sheila's by then notorious—or, if you felt otherwise, courageous—opposition to abortion. Beginning after the U.S. Supreme Court's Roe v. Wade decision in 1974, Uncle George and Aunt Sheila had written increasingly forceful polemics, arguing that abortion revealed modern liberalism's nihilistic and instrumental view of human life. I could not go there. For me abortion was a settled question. So as we had done all our lives, the conservative uncle and his liberal nephew skated around the chasm that had opened up between our sides of the family.

He was saddened when I told him that his sister Alison—my mother—was now struggling with Alzheimer's disease, as their own mother had. There were tears in his eyes, but he said nothing, and I was left to wonder what moment of rupture between them had occurred in London so long before. There was no one else left to tell me, and to hold on to those memories of wartime London and his younger, intolerable self, now lost forever.

From there, I remember, our talk moved over to memories of his mother, Maude, and the fabled address, 7 Prince Arthur Avenue, where he had come home to rest and recover in 1942. We both remembered its bookcases and back pantry and carpeted sitting rooms, the water plants flowering in the battery jars by the windows, the silver cigarette cases on side tables, George Parkin's African animals on display shelves, every object holding out a promise that the past would be secure and unchanging and a place of refuge in time of trouble. In fact, of course, 7 Prince Arthur offered no such comfort. It had already been torn down, twenty years earlier.

I told him that I last remembered climbing into my grandmother's bed in 7 Prince Arthur, when I was seven or eight and she was about seventy-five. She wore a long flannel nightie buttoned at the neck, and her voluminous grey hair, usually pinned in a tight chignon, flowed loose and thick on the pillows. She had a breakfast tray on her lap, with a silver tea service and a plate of buttered Ryvita biscuits from England. I remember she gave me one to eat while she folded *The Times* of London, in its feather-light international edition, and read the death notices to me, remarking occasionally that she knew the deceased.

As I told him this—one single morning in my child-hood, and the last in which I had a direct connection with the traditions described in this book—Uncle George's face crumpled. He stood up and, clenching his fists close to his chest, exclaimed in a voice of pain and pure longing, "Oh God, I wish that had happened to me!" It took me aback to see this giant of a man so nakedly exposed in all his need and unresolved love of his mother, dead for twenty years. But I am glad to think back on it now, for it taught me—and I needed to know this—that family traditions are more than arguments with the dead, more than collections of family letters you try to decipher. A tradition is also a channel of memory through which fierce and unrequited longings surge, longings that define and shape a whole life.

George Grant lived five more years after that meeting, though I never saw him again. He died of cancer in 1988, at the age of seventy, and is buried in the graveyard at Terrence Bay, Nova Scotia, where he had built a cottage years before, because, he said, it seemed a holy place. His headstone reads: George Parkin Grant, 1918–1988. "Out of the Shadows and Imaginings into the Truth."

5

THE INHERITANCE

I

In July 2000, my wife, Zsuzsanna, and I set off to retrace my great-grandfather's original journey. We would have liked to take a steamer through the Great Lakes, but passenger boats stopped running on the lakes decades ago, so we flew to Thunder Bay and our journey began at the car rental counter at the airport.

I thought it would be hard to find any traces of George Monro Grant, but this country takes better care of its past than I expected. The old Hudson's Bay forts have been restored and turned into museums. Moccasins, blankets and trade beads are on sale in their stores. When the old homesteads are cleared away for a supermarket or a highway, they are jacked up onto a trailer, together with their split-rail fences, and they are set down, along with lots of other old buildings, in an interpretive centre. The buildings may have the forlorn look of animals in a zoo, but it's good to walk through the parlours of the old houses to get the feel of the dimensions in which our people once lived and died.

Governments, too, have done their part to preserve the past. In the 1960s, the federal government put up sturdy red brass plaques in the two official languages at many of our national heritage sites—and provincial governments followed suit and municipalities put up theirs, too. We've kept up the remains. There's a lot to show the kids.

It's relatively easy to find the old Dawson Road, even when it snakes through forest, way off the beaten track. The road leads you to Kakabeka Falls, which Grant and Fleming portaged around in July 1872. On the provincial park plaque, there was even a quotation from George Monro Grant informing tourists, though they hardly needed to be told, that the water tumbling off a shale ledge and then cascading into a narrow gorge a hundred feet below is indeed a magnificent sight.

Fleming and Grant helped to carry the birchbark freight canoes through the portage routes around those falls. Back in the water, of course, they sat in style in the middle with Ignace and Toma keeping up a stroke to the cry of "hi hi." We travelled in a rented Ford with country music on the radio. Travel was so easy for us that it was sometimes hard to feel the contours of the land that they struggled to master.

We followed their route, the old fur-trader trails through Fort Frances, now a pulp town, and wended our way along the highway to towns like Kenora and Sioux Lookout, stopping at the gas stations that sell fishing licences and rent boats. We passed signs pointing down gravel roads to reservation lands held by the descendants of the Ojibwa people my great-grandfather met in 1872.

On the long traverse of northwestern Ontario and the forested part of eastern Manitoba, the two-lane blacktop, etched into the rock of the Canadian Shield, plunged through deep forest cover. We thought we saw a baby bear disappearing into the bush by the side of the road. The radio would give us the news and more country music and then the signal would grow fuzzy and die away. You could imagine how hard it must have been to cover this terrain in a Red River cart rattling over a plank-covered forest trail.

When we burst through the forest cover, east of Winnipeg on the Trans-Canada, we felt some of the awe and wonder George Monro Grant felt that day in July 1872, as the big sky opened up above, the horizon widened out and the sun poured down on the vast prairie pastures all around us.

Near Winnipeg airport, we even found a prairie grass museum, about an acre of native flower–filled prairie grass, the same kind George Grant rode through on horseback, driving the plovers and bumblebees up into the air.

After Winnipeg, we picked up the Yellowhead route and threaded our way slowly through the small towns and farm lands of Manitoba and Saskatchewan. We took some wobbly video of each other in front of gas stations where semis, loaded with pipe and logs, were lined up for fuel. We stayed in small motels where we shared hot tubs or pools with truckers with sunburnt arms and faces. After some delicious roadhouse pie at a coffee shop in Manitoba, we decided to find the best homemade pie in the West.

In central Saskatchewan, near Saskatoon, we stopped at Wanuskewin, once a dry river gorge with steep cliffs where the Cree used to drive the buffalo and, having slaughtered their share, would gather for feasts and ceremonies. Now there is a museum full of headdresses, beaded jackets, moccasins and life-sized buffalo sculptures. The herds are gone, but on one of the ranches nearby, buffalo were being raised for slaughter, and we stopped to photograph the creatures munching grass behind barbed wire.

We took unpaved back roads wherever we could, a big plume of dust rising behind us, the only sound the rumble of the tires on the gravel. The canola was a warm shade of bright yellow and stood waist high in the fields. When we would get out of the car to stretch our legs, the thump of the door shutting behind us would echo for long seconds in the silence.

There were churches everywhere on those back roads, Ukrainian and Russian ones with onion domes, white wood-frame United churches with silver steeples, a few French Catholic ones with images of the Sacred Heart on the walls, visible through the window panes. All of them were very neat, with the grass trimmed and cut flowers decorating the graves in the cemeteries.

On a hillside above Esterhazy, Saskatchewan, Zsuzsanna—who is Hungarian—spent a long time among the headstones commemorating the Bartoks and Nagys, peasant families who were brought out in the 1880s by a CPR land agent called Count Esterhazy. He settled them on homestead plots and left them to fend for themselves. We visited a local museum and saw photos of the sod houses and the unsmiling women in kerchiefs standing outside them and the men with handlebar moustaches leaning on pitchforks, all of them burnt raw by the sun and the wind.

My great-grandfather had dreamed of these pioneers and of the western horizon they would create, with the smoke wafting from their homesteads, their land fenced out and under the plough. It had all come to pass. But the hard faces in the photographs made it clear that creating a home on the plains had been tougher than he had imagined.

From 1885 until the 1960s, all the settlement on the Prairies was strung out along the railroad tracks. But the railroad had long since ceased to serve as the spine of the country. The freights were still running, loaded with grain and pipe and potash, but the passenger trains had all but stopped. We met a former railwayman who cursed when he told us how they were smashing up the remaining passenger cars for scrap. The small western railway stations—stout, gabled brick buildings with sloping roofs that provided shade while you waited for the train—had been converted into restaurants or boutiques or were boarded shut.

In Manitoba and Saskatchewan people were leaving the farms and small towns and heading for Winnipeg, Regina and Saskatoon. Little towns were struggling. The old wooden grain elevators were being torn down. Stores were boarded up in main streets all across the West. The Canada that George Monro Grant had dreamed of was passing away, but a new Canada was taking shape in the downtown universities and research institutes, the law firms and the business parks.

The Canada that he thought was already doomed in 1885—Aboriginal, Metis, Cree and French—was still vividly present, especially so in one place. We found the crossing point on the South Saskatchewan River that Fleming and Grant had taken in August 1872. We crossed on a ferry hooked to a wire, which took us over the hundred yards of fast-running river in about ten minutes. They had forded the river with the horses, breasting the current waist high, laughing and wet because they couldn't find a boatman to take them across on a scow. There was supposed to be one, but he wasn't there that day.

The boatman working the crossing that summer, so the records tell us, was one Gabriel Dumont, Metis scout, guide and later rebel leader. The Grant-Fleming party also missed

Xavier Letendre, the Metis trader nicknamed Batoche, who was to build his trading post and liquor store on the river bank and whose name was given to the crossing place.

At Batoche we went up the hill and talked to the carpenters restoring the old plain plank church. We went over to the graveyard, the final resting places of the Cree and Metis who made their last stand here against Middleton's troops in 1885, the soldiers Macdonald had sent out on the railway. It was here that the army took Louis Riel prisoner. The photographs show him manacled, bare headed and unkempt, a broken visionary of a West that was Cree, Metis and French.

When we reached Edmonton, we headed straight out to West Edmonton Mall. My children—Theo and Sophie—had joined us by then and they had been told the mall was the largest in the world. There was a beach with plastic palms, terrifying (at least to me) water slides, a pirate ship in the middle of a supermarket and other wonders to behold. It took some doing to imagine that one hundred and twenty-eight years before, my great-grandfather had ridden into Fort Edmonton, nearby, and had himself photographed in his riding chaps and buckskin jacket.

From Edmonton, we made our way toward Jasper, where, after much searching up and down the river bank just out of town, we found the lobstick—the giant pine, its topmost branches cut away—and the rusty railway spike

Fleming and Grant had smashed into the gnarled base of the trunk.

West of Hinton, Alberta, on the Yellowhead Highway, we spent a night at the Black Cat Guest Ranch so we could do some horseback riding in the foothills. The shale tracks, through deep forest cover, leading to the Yellowhead Pass, had been the most exhausting stretch of the Fleming-Grant expedition. We spent a late afternoon on docile quarter horses, slowly going up the trails until we reached a summit with a view of the mountains ahead, their crags and peaks touched with golden light. While we were resting at the top, we heard a rumble and saw one hundred and forty boxcars—the children counted them—snaking through the gorge below us. The lonesome wail of a train whistle rose up in the evening air, echoing off the canyon walls.

In the days that followed, we crossed the Great Divide, drove through the Yellowhead Pass and began making our way down to the Pacific. We drove through the sagebrush country around Kamloops. We passed through the narrow river gorges where Grant had seen the sweat lodges of the river people. In the Fraser Canyon, we stopped for a cappuccino at a trading post where they sold bentwood boxes made by Aboriginal inmates at the local provincial prison.

We finally found the best pie of the journey—it was made from Okanagan peaches—at a Ukrainian family's café, somewhere along the Thompson River valley.

We doubled back through the Selkirk Mountains to Craigellachie. The kids clambered aboard the steam engine on the siding, and we toured the gift shop. You could buy pictures of Fleming and Smith, in their top hats, standing among the labourers as the last spike was driven in. Replicas of the last spike were on sale, some in bronze, some in inflatable plastic, but we didn't buy any.

Down the highway through the Fraser Valley, in driving rain, visibility close to zero, the trucks' backwash dousing our windscreen, we reached journey's end, in the auto shops, tract housing, malls and fast food restaurants of the Lower Mainland. When George Monro Grant arrived here in 1872, by steam launch down the Fraser, there had only been looming pines and silence broken by the keening of gulls.

He had seemed a close presence all along the way.

II

The Canada of the Grants was a small-town nation of modest brick houses with white verandas, Protestant and Catholic churches on wide, leafy streets and the railway station within walking distance. George Parkin Grant's *Lament for a Nation* was a cry of grief and rage at its passing. But that Canada is still there. Just go to Richmond, Quebec, or London, Ontario, or Halifax, Nova Scotia. There are beautiful streets in each of these towns where this Canada still remains. But there is a palpable sense that time is passing this Canada by.

A new Canada has been built up around it—condominium towers, suburban tract housing, shopping plazas, sixteen-lane highways and the multicultural bazaar of downtown. This is now our home and native land.

The Canada of the Grants may be slipping away, but their way of thinking about the country still offers enduring lessons. They believed in the country's future with an enthusiasm that can still inspire. They thought the country was unfinished, that there was a great nation still to be built. They thought that it ought to have a purpose and a meaning. They were romantics.

But there is more to their inheritance than romance.

They also understood the deeper logic of the country.

My great-grandfather and his generation—John A. Macdonald, Sandford Fleming and Donald Smith—were nation builders. They understood that Canada was called into being by an act of choice and that it could only be sustained by continual acts of political faith and willpower.

They understood that the political ties that bound the country together ran east and west but the economic ties that kept Canada going ran north and south. The political task in Canada, these ancestors understood, was to build steel rails and bonds of citizenship from east to west to hold the country together in the face of the economic and geographic ties running north and south. If the east–west links of steel and citizenship were strong enough, then the country could survive and prosper. This remains the logic of Canada to this day. If we want a country to hand on to the next generation, we will have to strengthen those east–west linkages—of citizenship and common life together—to offset the north–south drift that fragments us.

Are the east–west linkages strong enough to sustain us today? We have had free trade with the United States for twenty years, yet we still do not have free trade in labour and capital among Canadian provinces. We still do not maintain a single economic space from ocean to ocean. We still maintain barriers that prevent Canadians from doing business with each other or from pulling up stakes and moving where the work is. Our forefathers would not understand why we lack the will to pull them down.

The ribbon of steel that used to tie us together is almost gone. Now we have the airlines and the bus companies and we pretend to have a national highway. In many places—northern Ontario or the interior of British Columbia—it dwindles down to two-lane blacktop, and the local residents will tell you these narrow sections make our national highway a death trap. We could do better. The Americans completed a four-lane national highway system fifty years ago. We are still awaiting ours.

The Europeans have used high-speed railways to tie Europe together. After fifty years of studies, we are still considering a high-speed rail link to connect Windsor to

Quebec City, Vancouver to Calgary and Calgary to Edmonton. If we want to tie Canadians together, if we want to be nation builders, we would start on them right now. Here the nineteenth-century buccaneers—Fleming, Van Horne, Rogers, John A. himself—offer an example of the political grit and daredevil entrepreneurship that Canada has always called upon when it truly wants to achieve great things.

Those ancestors would look at our incredible panoply of resources in energy and say to us our work of nation building is not yet done.

They would want to know why so much of the oil and gas we produce flows south without even being processed. We ship oil from Alberta and Saskatchewan to the American states while importing large quantities from Venezuela and the Middle East to meet the demand in Ontario, Quebec and the Atlantic provinces. Does this make sense? Why are we one of the few countries that has never created a petroleum reserve to protect our citizens against fluctuations in supply from foreign countries? In the future opening up before us, our children will judge us harshly for having no apparent national energy strategy whatever.

It is possible we do this because we do not take ourselves seriously enough. My uncle George argued, like so many thinkers in the 1960s, that Canada was a mere branch plant of the United States. We are such captives of these worn-out clichés of dependency that we fail to grasp our newfound strength. We haven't noticed that times have changed and so have the terms of trade with our neighbour. Nowadays, we export more oil to the United States than Saudi Arabia does. If energy is power, then we ought to have plenty of it. We have cards to play at the table of nations, and if we play the energy card with determination, we can build a country that commands respect—the respect that comes from being not just a good neighbour but a powerful one, too.

These are not the only questions the ancestors would be asking.

We are one of the greatest producers of hydroelectric power in the world. Quebec's Quiet Revolution was paid for by its hydro. Why does so much of our hydro flow north to south rather than east to west? Why are the alternative energy sectors of our country—wind, solar and ocean power—crying out for more east–west grid capacity? Why can't we build energy corridors to move Manitoba power to Ontario, Ontario nuclear power to Quebec and the power from the Lower Churchill to central and Atlantic Canada? Why can't we develop a strategic vision of how to do this and then stick with it, over decades, until we have the national energy grid system we need?

These are the crucial issues of energy security, national independence and national unity that a Fleming, a Grant, a John A. Macdonald or a Laurier would have seen as clear as day. We might be tempted to tell them that energy flows north to south because it flows to market. That's the logic of money. But they would have waved this away with an impatient gesture. They would have told us the country wouldn't exist at all if the logic of money had determined our destiny. We'd be Americans.

So the question that they asked and answered, in their fashion, demands an answer in our time: What exactly is being Canadian worth to us, in dollars and cents? How much are we prepared to invest to keep our country in one piece?

*Ocean to Ocean—a Mare usque ad Mare—*encapsulated the national vision of the railway age. Our ancestors would be asking us: What is the national vision of our age?

The opening up of the Northwest Passage, once our frozen inland waterway, is an opportunity for Canada to develop a new frontier. Again, we do not appreciate the power we actually possess. As an Arctic nation, we are the sovereigns of a considerable portion of the world's refrigeration system. The future of the planet's weather depends on how we, along with other Arctic nations, stabilize this system and guarantee its future health for the benefit of the world.

It is true we are a difficult country to govern, as Laurier said. Caution and compromise are properly the essence of our politics. Our union is fragile. But it is equally true, as these nineteenth-century voices remind us, that we wouldn't exist at all if we hadn't also been a nation of gamblers and daredevils, the kind of people who don't take no for an answer. The ambition of our ancestors should be inspiring us to equal them in daring today and tomorrow.

III

As ministers of the cloth, school principals and professors—as the public intellectuals of their time—the Grants took it upon themselves to pose, and then to answer, the central question facing the country of their day.

For my great-grandfather's generation, the question was whether the Canada he grew up in, the five British colonies grouped along the St. Lawrence, could take possession of the West and transform itself into a continental nation-state. The answer, given after the journey in *Ocean to Ocean,* was yes.

For my grandfather's generation, the question was whether Canada could emancipate itself from the British Empire and achieve national independence. The answer, given at the Somme, at Vimy and at Passchendaele, was yes.

For my uncle's generation, the question was whether Canada, having emancipated itself from the British

Empire, could now survive as an independent state within the American Empire. The right answer—though not the one he gave—is yes.

The tradition of which I am part is an affirmation of Canadian possibility. But it is also a tradition that issues a challenge to the future. It asks the fourth generation to pose, in our turn, the key question about our country that we must answer.

The Grants understood that the question about Canada is what place it can make for itself in a world of empires. Today the challenge is how Canada maintains its sovereignty and identity in the vortex of a globalization that is beyond the control of a single empire.

The globalization the Grants understood was a benign creation of empire. My great-grandfather was never frightened by the pace of change or the violence of world events because he believed that the world was ordered by the flag, the navy and the crown. When Britain's imperial era came to an end, Canada shaped an identity in the shadow of American power.

My uncle George did his thinking in the imperial high noon of American power and believed that American rule would be eternal. In fact, no empire's rule is eternal, and we are living the end of that American noon hour. Over the past fifty years, the world's centre of gravity has shifted away from the North Atlantic, where it rested as Canada grew into nationhood, and has moved east to the Pacific and the Indian oceans.

These are the shifts in the tectonic plates that will define Canada's place in the world and its very identity. The question now is how Canada finds a new place in a world where it can no longer count on any imperial partner or protector, a world in which, as a consequence, Canada must look to itself to guarantee its sovereignty and the integrity of its way of life.

If the twenty-first century does not necessarily belong to America, then we owe it to ourselves to move out beyond North America and seek opportunities elsewhere, wherever we can find them. We owe it to ourselves to find other partners to build the kind of international order we need, with effective international law, responsible international development assistance and a fair world trading system. We cannot wait for the Americans or the Chinese. We should form our own coalitions of the willing—with European states and with developing democracies—and we should not be afraid to lead. This requires confidence in ourselves, but we should remember those ancestors of ours who fought for a Canadian place at the imperial gatherings that decided how the world would be ordered. We can surely do the same. The emerging world order of the twenty-first century is ours to shape and, to the degree that we play our part in shaping it, we can feel at home in it.

What Uncle George did understand was that no national identity, not even of great nations, is secure and beyond challenge in a world of unregulated and uncontrolled globalization. Canada's problem is not unique. Canada shares the same problem with larger nations, maintaining the integrity of its identity and citizenship in a globalizing economy that hammers away at the capacity of national institutions to deliver citizens control of their culture and their economy.

This is a world where decisions about who gets work and who doesn't, who prospers and who goes hungry, are made not by governments directly, but by the forces of a market that no single government or empire either controls or fully understands.

But government does still matter. Countries with good government can master globalization; countries with bad government will be its victims. George Grant's mistake was to abandon faith in ordinary politics and the capacity of his fellow citizens to shape their lives through free institutions. No country may be fully sovereign over its identity, but well-governed countries are more sovereign than others, more capable of mastering change and preserving the vital core of traditions, beliefs and values that give a people their identity. Well-governed countries maintain peace, order and good government at home. They punish crime; they hold their citizens accountable for basic standards of conduct. These successful countries run immigration programs that attract entrepreneurial and able people from around the world to become citizens. Bipartisan political consensus guarantees steady national investment in education and training, in science and technology, in infrastructure, and in the public goods that draw citizens together and help to make them productive. These successful countries knock down the barriers—of red tape, regulation and monopoly—that divide citizens, confer unfair advantages or prevent people from working together.

None of these successful countries is foolish enough to believe that it is a finished creation. They all take their promises of equality, fairness and justice seriously, which means that their leaders know that there are still promises to keep. These countries don't protect their markets against global competition; they invest in their own people's vision and enterprise so they can gain footholds in other people's markets. Above all, these successful countries keep their governments honest and accountable. Trust in government, faith in the people who are elected, belief that public policy can actually improve people's lives—these are the emotions that sustain the citizenship of successful societies.

Such societies are successful not just because they are prosperous and free, but because their citizens share a sense that they know where they came from and know where they are headed in the future. They are hopeful. They believe in themselves. They believe in the capacity of their people to do great things. They are patriots.

Patriotism—enduring, impatient, non-ironic belief in the promise of the land you love—is the single greatest asset of successful societies. Successful societies struggle with their deficiencies and overcome them through collective efforts of will and sacrifice. Patriotism is the sentiment that makes a people demand reform, change and improvement in their country; patriotism is the source of the impatience and anger that makes abuses intolerable, injustice unacceptable and complacency a delusion.

It is this sentiment that makes us want to be one people. It is this shared feeling that allows us to rise above our differences—English and French, Aboriginal, Metis, Inuit, immigrants from every land—and makes a complex unity of us all.

This unity, never certain, never to be taken for granted, always a work in progress, has meaning for us, but it also offers an example to others. Canadians know as much as anyone about living together across the gulf of great differences; we know how to compromise with each other and yet maintain what is essential; we know how to live with the differences that cannot be overcome. We have some experience in respecting the rights of individuals and yet also protecting the collectivities of language and culture that give individuality meaning. We know something, too, about a national pride that is ironic, modest, self-deprecating yet also robust. We know the difference between true patriot love and false, between love that always respects the truth of who we are, however painful, and the love that devours the truth and replaces it with lies. Most of all, we know—as some other nations do not—that the question of who we are is never settled and that we rise to our best when we allow ourselves to imagine ourselves anew.

NOTES

Abbreviations

George Monro Grant: GMG

Jessie Lawson Grant: JLG

Maude Parkin Grant: MPG

William Lawson Grant: WLG

George Parkin Grant: GPG

Jessie Alison Grant Ignatieff: JAG

Mary Greey: MG

Elisabeth Greey: EG

Chapter 2

p. 40 "dirty, joyless looking and prematurely old"
   G.M. Grant, *Ocean to Ocean* (1873), p. 38

p. 48 "a dignity of manner that whites" *Ocean to Ocean,*
   p. 88

p. 48 "any positive improvement" *Ocean to Ocean,* p. 138

p. 49 "keep the Lord's day after" *Ocean to Ocean,* p. 139

p. 53 "cleanly, orderly, patient, industrious"
   Ocean to Ocean, p. 301

p. 68 "we govern ourselves, yet are not independent"
   The Dominion of Canada, p. 242

p. 68 "patronizing language too often used"
   The Dominion of Canada, p. 558

p. 69 "there was nothing to do but fight it out"
   Queen's Quarterly, vol. 8, p. 236

p. 69 "we aspire to be a nation" *Queen's Quarterly,* vol. 7,
   p. 255

Chapter 3

p. 82 "I have come to love you very deeply"
   WLG to MPG, Kingston, 3 August 1910

pp. 83–84 "Will you always love me?"
   WLG to MPG, Kingston, 12–13 January 1911

p. 84 "we prate of our Canadian nationalism"
   WLG to MPG, Kingston, 9 February 1911

p. 85 "Christ" WLG to MPG, 2 April 1911

p. 87 "grips me, overwhelms me" WLG to MPG,
   London, 31 July 1914

p. 88 "Just then out came the King, Queen and Prince"
   WLG to MPG, July/August 1914

NOTES

p. 88 "fierce, hellish spirit of this war" WLG to MPG,
    August 1914

p. 89 W.L. Grant, *Our Just Cause* (1914)

p. 91 "just for the variety" WLG to MPG, Gananoque,
    3 February 1916

p. 91 "drunk and sober, rough necks and gentlemen"
    WLG to MPG, Gananoque, February 1916

p. 93 "I shall see Miss Allison Grant" WLG to MPG,
    Gananoque, 1916

p. 96 "Dearest, I yearn for you" WLG to MPG,
    somewhere in France, 7 August 1916

p. 96 "political, philosophical, military" WLG to MPG,
    France, August 1916

p. 97 "parapet" WLG to MPG, somewhere in France,
    8 August 1916

p. 98 "My dear Maude" WLG to MPG, somewhere in
    France, 17 August 1916

p. 100 "poor country cousin" WLG to MPG, London,
    12 December 1916

p. 101 "terrible and splendid" WLG to MPG, Kent,
    April 1917"

p. 112 "we both come of good blood my dear"
    WLG to MPG, Craigellachie, late 1918

Chapter 4

p. 124 "rather smug sense of admiration" JAG to GPG, 1940.

p. 126 "I helped wounded people" GPG to MPG, Bermondsey, January 1941

p. 127 "Granny Peck" GPG to MPG, Bermondsey, 27 December 1940

p. 127 "God I have learned more about loving" GPG to MPG, Bermondsey, late 1940/early 1941

p. 127 "black in the face with smut and dirt" Claude Bissell, *The Imperial Canadian* (1986), p. 13

p. 128 "marvellous job" William Christian, *George Grant: A Biography* (1993), p. 77

p. 129 "My railway arch was hit" GPG to MPG, Bermondsey, 22 January 1941

pp. 129–130 "tiger-like violence" and "brave new world" GPG to MPG, London, June 1941

p. 130 All other quotations, GPG to MPG, London, 15 June 1941

p. 130 "decided to enlist in the merchant marine" GPG to MPG, London, 21 August 1941

p. 133 "in 1940 we saw" George Grant, *Empire, Yes or No* (1945), p. 10

p. 136 "my need for God" GPG to MPG, Balliol College, 3 November 1945

NOTES

p. 137 "I love England" GPG to MPG, Balliol College,
    13 November 1945

p. 137 "you cannot have the plums after being a pacifist"
    GPG to MPG, Balliol College, 19 November 1946

p. 142 "a celebration of" George Grant, *Lament for a
    Nation* (2000), p. 7

pp. 142–143 "the character of Canada as British North
    America" *Lament for a Nation*, p. 33

p. 145 "Those who loved the older traditions" *Lament for
    a Nation*, p. 94–95

p. 146 "Hope in the future has been" Sheila Grant,
    William Christian (eds.), *The George Grant Reader*
    (1998), p. 88

PRIMARY SOURCES AND ACKNOWLEDGMENTS

The Grant Parkin Papers (MG 30 D77) in the National Archives of Canada were the major primary source for this book. I am grateful to the archivists at the National Archives for assisting me.

The Papers, which run to forty volumes, cover the lives and careers of George Monro Grant, William Lawson Grant, George Parkin and George Parkin Grant, as well as their wives and children. I am grateful, as all members of our family must be, to Raleigh Parkin, youngest brother of Maude Parkin Grant, for doing such valuable work, during his retirement, collecting letters and materials from members of the family and donating them to the National Archives.

Since this book was not intended as either a scholarly work or a full-scale family history, but rather as an intellectual history of their ideas of Canada, I made selective use of these voluminous archives: the letters of George Monro

Grant home to his wife, Jessie Lawson Grant, in 1872 and again in 1883; his letters home to her and to his sons during his world tour in 1888, and his correspondence with Sir Wilfrid Laurier during the Boer War crisis; the letters between William Lawson Grant and Maude Parkin Grant between 1910 and 1918; and finally, the letters between George Parkin Grant and Maude Parkin Grant between 1939 and 1941.

In addition, I consulted the Sandford Fleming Papers in the National Archives of Canada, in particular the Fleming diaries relating to his trip with George Monro Grant to the Rogers Pass in 1883.

I wish to thank the archivists at Upper Canada College for their help in locating College photographs of William Lawson Grant and for retrieving from the archives the complete set of his addresses to the school between 1918 and 1934.

The papers of George and Alison Ignatieff are located in the archives of Trinity College, University of Toronto. I wish to thank the archivist for locating a number of letters by my mother to my father in 1945.

I also benefited from the kindness of Laura Brandon of Ottawa, who made available to me the correspondence between her mother, Mary Greey, her aunt Elizabeth Greey and Alison and George Grant between 1939 and 1941.

Every member of the Grant-Parkin-Andrew-Ignatieff families owes a particular debt of gratitude to William Christian, formerly of the University of Guelph, now retired, whose biographies of George Parkin Grant and Sir George Parkin have helped us all to understand these complex figures in our own past. Christian's superb chapter on George Grant's wartime experiences was particularly helpful to me.

I wish to thank Alana Fischer, formerly of the Carr Center for Human Rights Policy at the Kennedy School of Government, Harvard University, for her valuable research in 2005 and Trevor Harrison for his help in securing papers from the National Archives and for his valuable work in compiling the notes.

My brother, Andrew Ignatieff, read the manuscript and shared with me his memories of characters we both knew. I am grateful for his astonishing loyalty and unstinting friendship.

University College at the University of Toronto honoured me with an invitation to give the Priestly Lectures in 2008 and I thank the Principal and the College for allowing me to give an earlier version of these chapters as lectures.

Kay Gimpel (née Moore) shared 54A Walton Street with my mother and was kind enough to share her memories of London in wartime. I thank Kay for her devoted friendship both to my mother and to me.

Michael Levine, friend, agent, lawyer and counselor over thirty years, kept faith in this project while it lay dormant in my mind and helped me bring it to fruition.

The editorial team at Penguin, led by Diane Turbide, and the team at Boreal, led by Pascal Assathiany, showed understanding and forbearance toward the author throughout the production process.

My greatest debt of gratitude is to my wife, Zsuzsanna, to whom this book, like all my books, is dedicated.

Secondary Sources

Barris, Ted. *Victory at Vimy: Canada Comes of Age, April 9–12, 1917.* Toronto: Thomas Allen, 2007.

Bercuson, David J. & Granatstein, J.L. *Dictionary of Canadian Military History.* Toronto: Oxford University Press, 1992.

Berger, Carl. *The Sense of Power: Studies in the Ideas of Canadian Imperialism, 1867–1914.* Toronto: University of Toronto Press, 1970.

Berton, Pierre. *Marching as to War: Canada's Turbulent Years, 1899–1953.* Toronto: Doubleday Canada, 2001.

Berton, Pierre. *The Promised Land: Settling the West, 1896–1914.* Toronto: McClelland & Stewart Ltd., 1984.

Bissell, Claude. *The Imperial Canadian: Vincent Massey in Office.* Toronto: University of Toronto Press, 1986.

Blaise, Clark. *Sir Sandford Fleming and the Creation of Standard Time.* London: Weidenfeld & Nicolson, 2000.

Carter, Sarah. *Aboriginal People and Colonizers of Western Canada to 1900.* Toronto: University of Toronto Press, 1999.

Cavanaugh, Catherine & Mouat, Jeremy, eds. *Making Western Canada*. Toronto: Garamond Press, 1996.

Cayley, David. *George Grant in Conversation*. Toronto: Anansi, 1995.

Cook, Ramsay. *The Regenerators: Social Criticism in Late Victorian English Canada*. Toronto: University of Toronto Press, 1985.

Christian, William. *George Grant: A Biography*. Toronto: University of Toronto Press, 1993.

Christian, William. *Parkin: Canada's Most Famous Forgotten Man*. Toronto: Blue Butterfly Books, 2008.

·Dyck, Harvey L. & Krosby, H. Peter, eds. *Empire and Nations*. Toronto: University of Toronto Press, 1969.

English, John. *Shadow of Heaven: The Life of Lester Pearson, Volume One, 1897–1948*. Toronto: Lester and Orpen Dennys, 1989.

Ewart, K.C., & John, S. *Canada and British Wars*. Ottawa. n.d.

Fleming, Sandford. *Canadian Pacific Railway: Report of Progress on the Explorations and Surveys Up to January 1874*. Ottawa: MacLean, Roger, & Co., 1874.

Fleming, Sandford. *The Intercolonial: Historical Sketch of the Inception, Location, Construction and Completion of the Line of Railway Uniting the Inland and Atlantic Provinces of the Dominion: with maps and numerous illustrations*. Montreal: Dawson Bros., 1876.

Fleming, Sandford. *England and Canada: A Summer Tour Between Old and New Westminster*. Montreal: Dawson Bros., 1884.

Grant, George. *The Empire, Yes or No.* Toronto: The Ryerson Press, 1945.

Grant, George. "Protest and Technology" in Charles Hanly (ed.) *Revolution and Response: Selections from the Toronto International Teach-In.* Toronto: McClelland & Stewart Ltd., 1966.

Grant, George. *Technology and Empire: Perspectives on North America.* Toronto: Anansi, 1969.

Grant, George. *English Speaking Justice.* Toronto: Anansi, 1974.

Grant, George. *Lament for a Nation: The Defeat of Canadian Nationalism.* Montreal: McGill-Queen's University Press, 2000.

Grant, George Monro. *Ocean to Ocean: Sandford Fleming's Expedition Through Canada in 1872.* Toronto: James Campbell, 1873.

Grant, George Monro. "The Dominion of Canada" in J.G. Holland (ed.) *Scribner's Monthly, an Illustrated Magazine for the People, Volume XX.* New York: Scribner & Co., 1880.

Grant, George Monro. *Picturesque Canada: The Canada As It Was and Is,* 2 vols. Toronto: Belden, 1882.

Grant, George Monro. *Queen's Quarterly,* vol. 7 (1899).

Grant, George Monro. *Queen's Quarterly,* vol. 8 (1900).

Grant, Sheila & Christian, William. *The George Grant Reader.* Toronto: University of Toronto Press, 1998.

Grant, William Lawson, & Hamilton, Frederick. *Principal Grant.* Toronto: Morang & Co. Ltd., 1904.

Grant, William Lawson. *Our Just Cause: Facts about the War for Ready Reference.* London: Heinemann, 1914.

Graves, Donald E. *Fighting for Canada: Seven Battles, 1758–1945.* Toronto: Robin Brass Studio, 2000.

Hill, Douglas. *The Opening of the Canadian West.* London: William Heinemann Ltd., 1967.

Horn, Bernd, ed. *Forging a Nation: Perspectives on the Canadian Military Experience.* St. Catharines, Ontario: Vanwell Publishing Limited, 2002.

Howard, Richard B. *Upper Canada College, 1829–1979.* Toronto: Macmillan, 1979.

Mackintosh, W.A. *The Economic Background of Dominion– Provincial Relations.* Toronto: McClelland & Stewart Ltd., 1939.

Marteinson, John. *We Stand on Guard.* Montreal: Ovale Publications, 1992.

Massey, Vincent. *What's Past Is Prologue: The Memoirs of Vincent Massey.* Toronto: Macmillan, 1958.

McQueen, Donald R., & Thomson, William D. *Constructed in Kingston: A History of the Canadian Locomotive Companies 1854–1968.* Kingston: Canadian Railroad Historical Association Publication, 2000.

Miller, Carman. *Painting the Map Red: Canada and the South African War, 1899–1902.* Montreal: McGill-Queen's University Press, 1993.

Miller, Carman. *Canada's Little War.* Toronto: James Lorimer & Co. Ltd., 2003.

Milton, Viscount & Cheadle, W.B. *The Northwest Passage by Land*. Toronto: Prospero Books, 2001.

Morris, P.C., Alexander. *The Treaties of Canada with the Indians of Manitoba and the Northwest Territories*. Toronto: Willing & Williamson, 1880.

Morton, Desmond. *Ministers and Generals: Politicians and the Canadian Militia, 1868–1904*. Toronto: University of Toronto Press, 1970.

Owram, Doug. *Promise of Eden: The Canadian Expansionist Movement and the Idea of the West, 1856–1900*. Toronto: University of Toronto Press, 1980.

Page, Robert. *The Boer War and Canadian Imperialism: Booklet no. 44*. Ottawa: Canadian Historical Association, 1987.

Pearson, Lester B. *Mike: The Memoirs of the Right Honourable Lester B. Pearson, Volume One, 1897–1948*. Toronto: University of Toronto Press, 1972.

Pitts, Jennifer. *A Turn to Empire: The Rise of Imperial Liberalism in Britain and France*. Princeton: Princeton University Press, 2005.

Preston, Richard A. *Canada and "Imperial Defense."* Durham, N.C.: Duke University Commonwealth-Studies Center, 1967.

Reid, Brian A. *Our Little Army in the Field: The Canadians in South Africa 1899–1902*. St. Catharines, Ontario: Vanwell Publishing Limited, 1996.

Ritchie, Charles. *Undiplomatic Diaries, 1937–1971.* Toronto: McClelland & Stewart Ltd., 2008.

Sharp, Paul F. *Whoop-Up Country: The Canadian-American West, 1865–1885.* Minneapolis: University of Minnesota Press, 1955.

Sprague, D.N. *Canada and the Métis, 1869–1885.* Waterloo, Ontario: Wilfrid Laurier University Press, 1988.

St. Germain, Jill. *Indian Treaty-Making Policy in the United States and Canada, 1867–1877.* Lincoln: University of Nebraska Press, 2001.

Taylor, Charles. *Radical Tories.* Toronto: Anansi, 1982.

Turner, Robert D. *West of the Great Divide: The Canadian Pacific Railway's First Century in British Columbia.* Winlaw: Sononis Press, 2003.

Vance, Jonathan F. *Unlikely Soldiers: How Two Canadians Fought the Secret War Against Nazi Occupation.* Toronto: HarperCollins, 2008.

Ward, Peter W. *White Canada Forever: Popular Attitudes and Public Policy Toward Orientals in British Columbia.* Montreal: McGill-Queen's University Press, 1990.

Warren, William. *History of the Ojibway Nation.* Minneapolis: Ross & Haines, 1957.

Willison, John. *Sir George Parkin: A Biography.* London: Macmillan, 1929.

INDEX

Aboriginal peoples
    Canada's impact on, 46, 48–49, 57, 59, 160, 164
    in Canadian national myth, 13, 23, 148, 162
    GMG encounters with, 38–41, 43, 47–50, 53, 56,
        57, 159
    residential schools, 50
    and Riel, 44, 59, 163
    treaty relationship with, 17
    See also Metis
abortion, 151
Allen, Sheila (wife of GPG), 137, 150–51
Andrew, Geoffrey, 119

Berlin, Isaiah, 4, 149
Bermondsey, 125–32, 134, 136, 144
Bickersteth, Burgon, 128, 137
Boer War, 21, 65–70, 77–78
Borden, Robert, 84, 92

Bourassa, Henri, 69

Britain and British Empire, 26–27, 102, 150
    after World War II, 140
    and the Boer War, 67–70, 77–78
    Canada as dependent upon, 21, 147–48
    and World War I, 88

British Columbia, 19, 36, 53–54, 57, 76, 164

British Commonwealth, 101, 133

British Military Intelligence (MI5), 135

Buchenwald, 135

buffalo, 46, 59, 160

Callaghan, Morley, 132

Canada Pension Plan (CPP), 148

Canadian Association of Adult Education, 132

Canadian Broadcasting Corporation (CBC), 25, 132

Canadian constitution, 148

Canadian flag, 149

Canadian identity
    and belief in Britain, 80, 93, 133, 138
    as a conservative nation, 133
    and globalization, 172, 174
    independence, 68, 101–2
    myths of origin, 11, 13, 23, 112, 148, 162
    railway in, 62, 167–68
    reinventing, 148–49, 170, 173, 176
    as a small-town nation, 165–66

and U.S., 11–13, 84, 142

effect of WWI, 93, 102, 111, 112

Canadian Pacific Railway (CPR), 45, 57, 62, 161

Canadian Shield, 37, 42, 159

Catholicism (Roman), 34, 140, 160, 165

Manitoba education, 44, 60–61

Champlain, Samuel de, 75

Charter of Rights and Freedoms, 148–49

Chinese Canadians, 53–54

Christian missionaries, 44, 48–49

citizenship

and bilingualism, 61

and cosmopolitanism, 6–7

dual, 13–14

east–west linkages of, 166–67

as service and sacrifice, 88

of successful societies, 175

and trust, 5

Cold War, 134, 149

Colonial Institute (London), 63

Confederation of Canada, 35–36

conscription (WWI), 92

Conservatives, 84, 142–43

Continental Divide, 52, 164

Cooperative Commonwealth Federation (CCF), 120

Craigellachie, 56, 59, 111, 165

Cree peoples, 43, 46, 47, 48–49, 57, 59, 160, 162, 163
Curtis, Lionel, 77–78

Dalhousie University (Halifax), 137, 140
Davies, Robertson, 107
Dawson Road, 38, 41, 158
Depression, the, 110
Diefenbaker, John, 141, 142
Dumont, Gabriel, 162–63

Edmonton, 50–51, 163
education
    as bilingual, 61
    break from British traditions, 103
    Manitoba schools crisis (1890), 60–61
    Ontario examination system, 105
    of working class, 77
English in Canadian national myth, 13, 23
Expo 67, 148

Fleming, Sandford, 20, 36–40, 57–59, 64, 138, 166, 168
Fraser Valley, 51, 52, 164, 165
free trade, 21, 149, 167
    trade reciprocity (1911), 84
French Canadians
    in Manitoba school system, 60–61
    in national myth, 13, 148

of the Prairie, 44–45, 59, 60, 162, 163

Riel's demands, 44

See also Québécois

Frontier College, 77, 105

globalization, 64, 149, 172, 174

Globe (Toronto), 60

Goring-on-Thames, 78, 80–81, 85–87, 90, 93, 99

Grant, Alison. *See* Ignatieff, Jessie Alison Grant (mother)

Grant, Charity, 86, 99, 119

Grant, George Monro (great-grandfather), 20, 23, 29–30, 35–36

   and the Boer War, 65–70

   death of, 70, 73

   early life of, 33–38

   on empire, 26, 62–63, 67–70

   on federal government, 61

   retracing journey of, 157–65

   a nationalist imperialist, 21

   a Presbyterian minister, 34–37

   as progressive and modern thinker, 138, 144

   second trip to the west, 57–58

   tour of British Empire, 62–67

   trip to South Africa, 65–66

   See also *Ocean to Ocean* (GMG); transcontinental crossing

Grant, George Parkin (uncle), 22–23, 25
  on abortion, 151
  on American imperialism, 133, 134, 137, 139, 143,
    146, 150
  birth of, 107–8
  Canada as lost in the past, 26
  on Canadian identity, 138
  a Christian conservative philosopher, 22, 137–46
  death of, 153
  death of mother, 141
  decision to enlist, 130–31
  on empire, 130
  fatalism of, 145–47
  on liberalism and the Liberals, 120–21, 139–40,
    141–44
  marriage of, 137
  on nuclear weapons, 133–34
  pacifism and World War II, 121–22, 125–34,
    133–34, 137, 138
  relationship with Alison, 122–23, 136, 152
  relationship with father, 110–11, 119, 120–21
  relationship with Ignatieffs, 25, 151–53
  relationship with mother, 119–20, 136, 153
  religious faith of, 132, 136–37, 144–45
  on Soviet Union, 133, 134
  unfit for service, 131
  The Empire, Yes or No, 133

"Have We a Canadian Nation?", 132–33

    See also *Lament for a Nation* (GPG)

Grant, James and Mary Monro, 33

Grant, Jessie Lawson (great-grandmother), 35, 67, 69, 73

    birth of son, 55

Grant, Margaret (aunt), 24, 86, 99, 119

Grant, Maude Parkin (grandmother), 74, 81–84, 84–85, 121, 132

    after William's death, 119

    birth of Jessie Alison, 91

    death of, 141

    Ignatieff's memories of, 152–53

    marriage, 85, 86

    during World War I, 90

Grant, William Lawson (grandfather), 20–21, 82, 83, 99

    academic achievements of, 76–77

    on belief in God, 85

    birth of, 55

    birth of Jessie Alison, 91

    death of, 110

    on empire, 27, 77–79, 80, 88, 93

    father's death, 73–75

    in France, 75

    on gender equality, 91

    marriage, 82–83, 85

    on patriotism, 109

    principal at UCC, 102–7, 106–7, 110

war, 88, 92, 94–99, 99–101
war, army life, 90–92
war, haunted by, 104–5, 110–11
war, reflections on, 108–9, 112–13, 121
wounded, 98–99
History of Canada, 75–76, 105–6
Our Just Cause, 89
Principal Grant, 74
Greey, Elizabeth, 128
Greey, Mary, 128

Hart House (University of Toronto), 128, 137
Heinemann Publishers, 89, 99
Howe, C.D., 141
Howe, Joseph, 35, 86
Hudson's Bay Company, 38, 41, 45, 46, 157
hydroelectric power, 169

Ignatieff, George, 123, 134, 143
Ignatieff, Jessie Alison Grant (mother), 24, 99, 119
Alzheimer's disease, 141, 152
birth of, 91, 93
effect of the war, 140
marriage, 20, 143
relationship with brother, 122–23, 136, 152
during the war, 128, 129, 132, 135

Ignatieff, Michael
    motivation for political life, 28–29
    relationship with GPG, 25, 150–53
    Russian political refugees, 18–20
    at Vimy monument, 113–15
    The Russian Album, 19
Ignatieff, Nicholas, 106, 123, 137
imagination
    Canada as invented, 11, 13, 14, 26, 177
    love of country as act of, 1–5
    and unity, 15–18
immigrants, 33, 55, 61, 161
    in Canadian identity, 6–7, 149, 166
    as citizens, 13–14
    and role of government, 174–75
    at UCC, 106–7
Imperial Federation League, 79–80
Imperial War Conference (1917), 101
Intercolonial Railway, 35–36
Iroquois guides, 38–41, 56

Jasper and railway spike, 51–52, 163–64

Kamloops, 53, 164
Kicking Horse River valley, 57–58
King, Mackenzie, 120

Lament for a Nation (GPG), 22–23, 25, 27–28, 134, 142–50, 165
  as a break from family values, 144–45
  reception of, 143–44
  wrongness of, 147–50
language
  bilingualism, 40, 44, 61, 148
  Canada and United States, 12
  and citizenship, 3
  in defining a country, 11
  diversity of, 15, 16
  French methods of teaching, 103
  in identity, 12
  Iroquois, 39
Laurier, Wilfrid, 20, 59, 69, 84, 92, 170
League of Nations, 22, 109
Letendre, Xavier (Batoche), 163
Liberal Party
  and Canadian identity, 148–49
  on conscription (World War I), 92
  defeat Diefenbaker, 141
  on trade reciprocity (1911), 84

Macdonald, John A., 20, 36, 59, 73, 163, 166, 168
Macdonnell, Jim, 96, 122, 128
MacMillan, Ernest, 106

Manitoba, 43, 44, 159, 160, 162
    schools crisis (1890), 60–61
    See also Winnipeg
Massey, Lionel, 130
Massey, Vincent, 75, 100, 102, 120, 122, 123, 137, 140
    marriage, 94
Mazzoleni, Ettore, 106
McMaster University, 140
medicare, 13, 147, 148
Metis, 44, 59, 148, 162, 163, 176
    on transcontinental expedition, 38–41, 46–47, 50,
        51, 56, 57, 111
    See also Aboriginal peoples
Milner, Lord Alfred, 77–78, 79
Moberly, Walter, 51–52
Moore, Kay, 132, 135
multiculturalism, 6–7, 166

national anthem, 3, 149
    French and English versions of, 16–17
    parodies of patriotism and, 8–9
    sense of citizenship, 4
    at Vimy monument, 115
national energy strategy, 168
national heritage sites, 157–58, 159, 160
New Brunswick, 76

North Atlantic Treaty Organization (NATO), 134

Northwest Passage, 170

Nova Scotia, 33, 35–36

nuclear weapons, 133, 141

Ocean to Ocean (GMG), 21, 25, 36–37, 111
 national vision of, 170, 171
 publication of, 55–56
 Riel's absence from, 44

oil, 168

Ojibwa peoples, 39–41, 43, 47, 159

Orangemen, 44, 59, 93

Ottawa, 28, 86, 143

Otter Lake, 24, 108

Oxford, 22, 76, 77, 78, 121, 136

Oxford and Bermondsey Club, 125, 126

Oxford English Dictionary, 63–64

Parkin, Alice (Massey) (Aunt Lal), 80, 94, 122, 127–28,
 129

Parkin, George R. (great-grandfather), 74, 87, 99, 121
 death of, 108
 on imperialism, 78–80
 visit to South Africa, 24, 80, 152

Parkin, Marjorie (Macdonnell), 80, 96

Parkin, Raleigh, 80, 90, 94

Parkin and Grant family heritage, 138

patriotism

    contested emotion, 5

    of family tradition, 14, 18, 122, 139, 142

    nationalism as false, 109

    parodies of, 8–9

    of successful societies, 176

    truth in morality of, 10

    of war, 88

peace, order and good government, 55, 174

Pearson, Lester "Mike," 123, 128, 129, 134, 140, 141, 142, 143

Pickersgill, Frank, 135–36

prairie churches, 160–61

prairie grass museum, 159

Presbyterianism, 20, 34, 45, 48, 56, 66, 139

Prince Arthur Avenue, 24, 132, 152

Protestantism, 44, 59–60, 60–61, 64, 110, 140, 165

provincial parks, 158

provincial relations, 167

Quebec

    and Boer War, 69–70

    hydroelectric power of, 169

    identity, 148

    on the railway, 60

    Riel, 59

on trade reciprocity (1911), 84
vision of Canada, 112
Québécois, 15–16, 92–93
See also French Canadians
Queen's University (Kingston), 20, 23, 56–57, 73, 82, 85–86, 119
Quiet Revolution, 148, 169

railway, transcontinental, 111, 138, 170
building of, 20, 56–58
east–west linkages of, 62, 167–68
effect of, 59–60, 161–62
last spike, 56, 58–59, 165
See also transcontinental crossing
Red River carts, 41, 45, 159
Rhodes, Cecil and scholarship, 67, 74, 76, 78–79, 80
George Ignatieff, 123, 143
Riel, Louis, 43–44, 59, 163
right to bear arms, 12, 147
Ritchie, Charles, 123, 140
Roe v. Wade, 151
Rogers Pass and A.B. Rogers, 57–58
Roosevelt, Franklin D., 120–21, 124
Rousseau, Jean-Jacques, 151
Royal Colonial Institute, 86, 88–89
Royal Society of Canada, 151

St. Andrew's College (near Toronto), 74, 75, 92

St. Boniface, 43–44, 61

St. Laurent, Louis, 141

Saskatchewan, 48, 159–62, 162–63

Sioux peoples, 40, 47–48

smallpox, 48, 53

Smith, Donald Alexander (Lord Strathcona), 45, 58–59, 68–69, 166

South Africa, 65–70, 78, 79

Statute of Westminster (1931), 102

Taché, Alexandre-Antonin (Archbishop of St. Boniface), 44–45

technology, 26, 64, 175
  nuclear weapons, 133
  resistance to, 27, 138, 142, 144, 146

Thunder Bay (Port Arthur), 38

Trans-Canada Highway, 42, 159, 167

transcontinental crossing, 20, 37–55
  effect on Aboriginals, 40–41, 46, 48–50, 53
  expedition members, 38–39
  Fleming's idea, 36
  Ignatieff retraces, 157–65
  route of, 37–38, 50, 54–55
  See also *Ocean to Ocean* (GMG)

Turner, R.E.W., 102

United Nations, 134
United States
  Canada compared to, 11–13, 55
  Canada's influence on, 124
  Canada's relationship with, 21, 147–48, 168–70, 172
  Grant-Parkin opinions of, 144–45
  imperialism of, 133
  influence on Canada, 141
  trade with Canada, 21, 84, 149, 167
  as victor of WWII, 140
University of Toronto, 146
Upper Canada College (Toronto), 23–24, 119
  George Parkin, 74, 108

Vancouver, 54
Victoria, 55

Weil, Simone, 139
Weizmann, Chaim, 81
West Edmonton Mall, 163
Willison, John, 108
Winnipeg, 159, 162
  Fort Garry, 42, 43, 44, 47
Workers' Educational Association (WEA), 77, 105
World War I, 22, 27, 87–88, 90–99, 94–99
  and British Empire, 90, 101–2
  conscription, 92

Somme, 22, 94, 122, 171

Vimy, 101, 103–4, 106, 115, 171

Vimy monument, 112–15

World War II, 22

bombing of London, 125–27, 128–29, 134

Canadians defending Britain, 123–24

invasion of Russia, 130

Pearl Harbor, 131

U.S. as victor of, 140

Yellowhead Pass, 52, 56, 159, 164

Yellow Quill reservation, 14